KU-876-271

MAKE YOUR OWN
CURTAINS AND CUSHIONS

CAVENDISH HOUSE

Does your home need a quick face-lift? Are you furnishing on a shoe-string budget? Perhaps you are simply bored with the same old decor for your chairs and windows. The answer to all these problems is contained in *Make Your Own Curtains and Cushions*, bright, practical and packed with lots of imaginative ideas to enliven your environment without spending a fortune. Even if you have never made your own cushions and curtains before, you can learn all the necessary techniques without difficulty, plus some really handy hints on how to estimate quantities, how to cut out different shapes, and how to sew basic seams.

You don't even need a sewing maching – if you're prepared to spend a little extra time on the longer seams, you can still produce fabulous results by following the same instructions. Why not start off with some simple cushions? You'll soon want to go on to the more challenging projects. All the steps are clearly illustrated with useful diagrams, and in addition there is invaluable information on the best sort of fabrics to use, how to choose the most suitable headings for curtains, and how to line and hang them.

Deciding on the appropriate look for a room can be a problem too, and we show you how to utilize different styles from the daringly modern to the elegant classic approach. You can change the atmosphere of a room to an amazing extent by introducing an entirely new window vista, or scattering a myriad-coloured pile of cushions on a couch. Try a fresh-as-morning look with a pair of crisp, see-through curtains, or make some gorgeous patchwork cushions in luxurious silk. We even show you how to make some simple roller blinds at a fraction of the price in the stores. Also, we've remembered the children – they'll fall in love with the collection of friendly zoo animals, and snuggle happily into a giant squashy floor cushion. *Make Your Own Curtains and Cushions* will help you transform your home, and provide you with a creative outlet for your leisure hours.

Edited by Yvonne Deutch

© Marshall Cavendish Limited 1972, 1973, 1974, 1975, 1976, 1983

Published by Marshall Cavendish Books Limited, 58 Old Compton Street, London W1V 5PA.

First printing 1976 (softback)
Second printing 1983 (hardback)

Printed by L.E.G.O., Vicenza, Italy

ISBN 0 86307 063 9

N.B. US terminology is indicated in the text by ( ) brackets

Contents

Pictures supplied by:
John Bethell 4T.
Steve Bicknell 31,33,38/9,40,44/5,56/7, 58/9,59.
J. P. Broad/R. McEvoy 22/3.
Camera Press 1.
Heidede Carstensen 4B,15.
Conway Picture Library 2CR,8.
Roland di Centa 2CR.
Alan Duns 34.
Du Pont Fabrics 2T.
Femina/Cousett & Huber 10.
Roger Gain 37.
International Wool Secretariat 37.
Peter Kibbles 27.
Chris Lewis 20,46,47,49,60,62.
Dawn Marsden 25.
Nigel Messett 6,16.
Brian Morris 2BL,37,42.
Peter Pugh Cook 52.
Josephine Rankin 14.
Ruffelette 11,12,13.
Sandersons Triad 7.
Rupert Watts 18,19.

Introduction

One of the quickest and most economical ways of giving a new look to a home is by the imaginative use of curtains and cushions. The cost of ready made soft furnishings is becoming prohibitive, and now that a wide variety of attractive fabrics is available, it makes sense to learn the few basic techniques.

Basic techniques

Plain sewing is the only basic skill needed to make the majority of designs included in the following pages. The main seams used are flat fell and French seams, and they are both very easy to learn. Also included are instructions on how to make piping, a useful method of making attractive and firm edges on cushions. Another requirement is some knowledge of how to estimate quantities of fabrics for the different types of curtains and cushions. Where you are following a specific pattern, the measurements are

already provided, however you will frequently need to make an estimate yourself, and the various methods are clearly explained.

Tools and equipment

If you already sew, you will probably have all the equipment you need on hand. On the last page, a list of useful accessories is given, with explanations of their use, although you may not need all these. However many tools you have, they should be kept in first class condition. It is pointless to buy an expensive pair of scissors, and then use them to cut everything from fuse wire to paper. Needles should be kept shining bright – there is nothing more irritating than trying to sew a seam with one that is rusted. If you are fortunate enough to own a sewing machine, make sure that it is properly serviced, and that you are familiar with all its attachments. If you have a leaflet, read it right through, and follow all the instructions supplied by the

manufacturer for the general care of the machine. If you are sewing by hand, you simply follow the same pattern instructions, but allow yourself a little extra time for longer seams. In general, the best policy is to organize whatever equipment you have in a sensible manner. Store needles, threads, tape measures, thimbles etc so that they are easily visible, not all jumbled together in the bottom of your sewing basket. Transparent plastic boxes with firm covers are available in a variety of shapes and sizes, and are ideal for storage.

Choosing fabrics

One of the most exciting aspects of making your own cushions and curtains is the range of fabrics available now in the stores. Some manufacturers have wide ranges of co-ordinated wallpapers and fabrics, many of them in very attractive designs and colours. Advice on choosing appropriate fabrics for curtains and cushions is amply supplied.

1

Basic seams

Plain seam
With right sides together, machine or backstitch to the distance of the seam allowance from edge of fabric.

Finishing seams
Either use the zig zag on your machine or turn the raw edge of seam allowance under and machine or hand stitch close to edge.

Flat fell seam
Join as for a plain seam and trim one side of seam allowance to within 6mm (¼in) of stitching line. Turn over raw edge to the other side and fold over trimmed edge. Tack (baste) and machine near the edge.

French seam
With wrong sides facing, pin and stitch seam 6mm (¼in) from seamline inside seam allowance. Trim close to stitching and lightly press stitched seam towards front. Turn article inside out. Working on wrong side, pin tack (baste) and stitch along original seamline, encasing raw edges in seam.

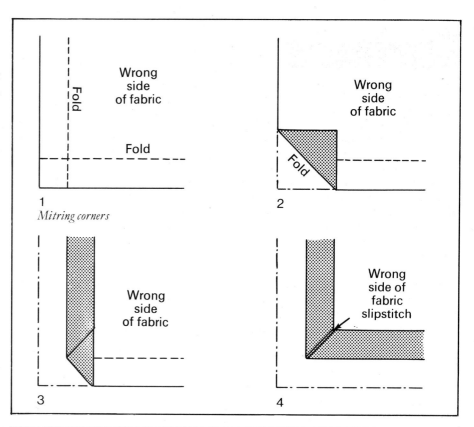

Mitring corners

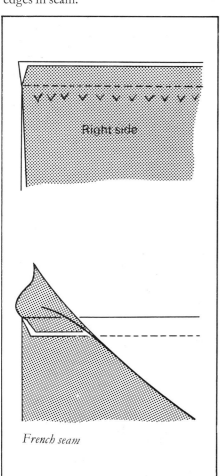

French seam

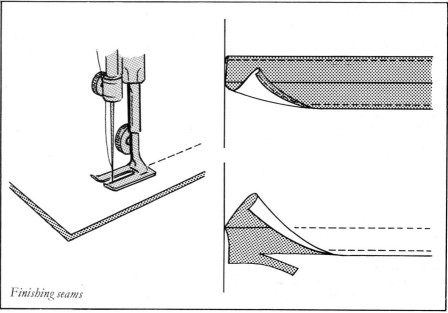

Finishing seams

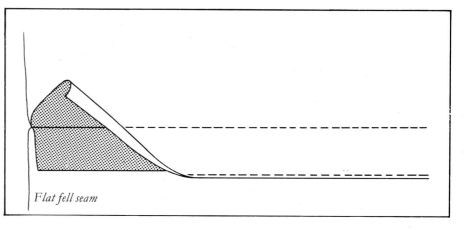

Flat fell seam

Curtains

Curtains have two main functions—first, to screen windows at night, giving privacy to lighted rooms and shutting out the darkness; and second, to form part of the room's decoration, by softening the hard outline of the windows during the day and by becoming an expanse of wallcovering at night when they are closed. To decide on the style of curtaining, have a good look at your windows in relation to the room and its other furnishings. Curtains can enhance or disguise the shape of windows and, if the window is out of proportion to the rest of the room, you can alter its apparent shape or size by adjusting the position of the curtain track. If daylight is restricted, the maximum amount of glass should remain uncovered when the curtains are drawn back. For this reason it is usually better to hang curtains outside reveals, but if you do have to hang them inside, take the track right round to the sides of the reveals so that no light is lost.

Sash windows

Double-hung sash windows—common in Britain in Georgian, Victorian and Edwardian houses—tend to be narrow and tall, often in rooms with high ceilings, so they look splendid with heavy, floor-length curtains. To make the windows appear wider, the curtain track should extend either side of the window so that the curtains can be pulled right back.

Casement windows

Casement windows can be of all sizes, with two, three of more sashes, but they are usually not very high, nor in high-ceilinged rooms. Full-length curtains can give them importance in a living room. Often they have to be ruled out, however, because of the siting of a radiator. Or, because many casement windows with two or three sashes are only about half the height of the walls, full-length curtains look odd when drawn back—and furniture cannot be pushed against the wall under the window, which is a snag in a small room.

Picture and pivot windows

Curtains for these should be full and heavy, so they drape well, and should have a decorative heading rather than a pelmet. Instructions for making these are given on page 11.

Top *A 'sham' curtain breaks up the broad window expanse.* **Above left** *Where the window is small, take the curtain track around on to the side wall.* **Above right** *A lace curtain adds an elegant touch to French doors, and is heavy enough to screen the room from sunlight if necessary.* **Left** *If you are fortunate enough to have a gracious room like this, with tall sash windows, you can use magnificent draped-swag curtain headings.*

Estimating curtains

Curtain fabric (standard headings)
The width of fabric needed depends on the weight of the fabric but varies between 1½ to 2 times the track length. Lighter fabrics look better with more fullness. So, depending on fabric, measure length of curtain track and multiply by 1½ to 2 (for double fullness). To this add 5cm (2in) on each side for hems. Add a further 15.3cm (6in) to each curtain width if they are to overlap in the centre. Total is width of fabric needed for a pair of curtains. For windows more than 1.2m (4ft) wide, fabric must be joined for width needed for gathering.
To measure length, use steel tape or yardstick. Measure length from curtain

Above *Sheer curtains are ideal for letting in the maximum light. Here they lend a graceful line to the contours of a room where the main feature is the beautiful ceiling.*

Left *Full length net curtains falling into gentle folds make a window space look light and airy, where a heavier curtain would tend to be bulky.*

track to either window sill or floor. Add 15.3cm (6in) for a double 7.6cm (3in) hem and 6.4cm (2½in) for a standard gathered heading. This measurement, multiplied by the number of widths required will give you the length of fabric needed for a pair of curtains. If you choose a pattern with a large repeat, extra will have to be allowed for matching. As a general rule you will need an extra pattern repeat for each curtain length. Check that washable fabrics are shrink-resistant, otherwise add about 2.5cm (1in) per foot of curtain length.

Estimating tie-backs

Loop the tape measure round curtain as if it were a tie back. Measurement of the loop is length of finished tie back. Straight tie backs would take about 22.9cm (¼yd) of curtain fabric or straight braid, 6.4cm (2½in) wide to required length, plus 2.5cm (1in) turning allowance. Also 22.9cm (¼yd) each of heavy buckram or pelmet buckram, interlining and lining. 4 brass curtain rings and 2 cup hooks. For shaped tie backs, draw pattern of shape required. Measure length of tie back as before, then halve this measurement. Draw pattern on brown paper folded as in diagram. Leave 7.6cm (3in) clear all around for turnings. Length and depth of opened out pattern will give amount of fabric needed for each tie back. Add same quantities of buckram, interlining and lining, rings and hooks.

Estimating café curtains

Decide on the finished length of the curtain. Café curtains usually cover half the window, but sometimes two curtains are used, one for the top half of the window and one for the lower half.
This type of curtain usually hangs to the sill or just below. To find the curtain width measure the track with a yardstick or steel ruler. Allow about 1½ times the length of track if a lined curtain with a scalloped heading is being used. For unlined curtains or those with more decorative headings, allow 1½ to 2½ times length of track. As for conventional curtains width needed depends on weight of fabric, lighter fabrics look better with more fullness.
To calculate the fabric length allow 15.3cm (6in) for lower hems and appropriate allowances for standard or deep heading tapes. For scalloped headings, decide on depth of scallop and add this measurement, plus 7.6cm (3in) for turnings, to curtain length. Remember to allow for design repeats if using

patterned fabric.
Linings. For sewn-in linings, you will need the same amount as for curtains, without allowance for pattern repeats. Lining fabrics are 1.2m (48in) wide. Check that the lining is pre-shrunk.
For detachable linings, cut linings the same size as the curtains, minus heading allowance and allowance for pattern repeats.
Heading tapes. Allow width of each curtain, plus 5cm (2in) for turnings. On lining tapes, allow 7.6cm (3in) extra. Before cutting pinch pleating tape, pleat up in arrangement you have chosen, check that finished length of tape is correct for curtain track.
Draped curtains. The side of the curtain which forms the drape will be longer than the side at edge of window. Use a piece of string and drape in a curve to estimate this length. You may find it easier to experiment with a length of calico (muslin) before cutting fabric. Draped net curtains can be hung from either one curtain rod or two, overlapped fully at the top or only overlapped for two thirds of the way across top of window. Allow for these possibilities when estimating fabric. The lower half of the curtain which is tied back can be shaped and cut at the window to your own requirements.
Side frills are often used on draped net curtains. Measure along edge where frill is to be applied, add half again to this measurement, double for a really full frill, plus 1.3cm (½in) seam allowances. An effective finished width is 7cm (2¾in). So for a double frill, cut a strip 14cm (5½in) wide, plus 1.3cm (½in) seam allowances all around.

Curtain fabric (pleated headings)
Pencil (cartridge) pleats. Allow at least two-and-a-half times the width of curtain track. Allow 12.7cm (5in) for heading and 10.2cm (4in) for hem on each width of fabric.
Pinch pleats. Allow 13cm (5⅛in) for heading and 10.2cm (4in) for hem on each width.
Most manufacturers of the particular pleating tape being used will supply a quantities chart on request to help you decide the number of widths and amount of pleating tape needed. Approximately 2 to 2½ times width of track.
Box pleats. Allow three times curtain width.

Unlined curtains
Fabrics to choose
Some curtains look best with light

filtering through them and good fabrics for this are coarsely woven linen and other semi-sheers. It may be necessary to have a second, lightweight curtain close to the window if privacy at night is necessary. Furnishing fabrics usually measure between 1.2m and 1.3m (48 and 50in) wide, while sheers and nets come in widths from 91.4–304cm (36 to 120in) wide.

Cutting and seaming
Widths of fabric seamed together must have perfectly matched patterns. The design must run continuously across the window and flowers should grow upward. Remember all the windows in the room must match. Try and finish curtains with a whole pattern if possible. Place fabric on a large flat surface for cutting. Straighten one end by drawing a thread through and cutting along the line. Measure and mark with pins for first width. Fold fabric along line marked with pins and cut along fold. Match pattern if necessary, then cut off second width in same way. Continue until all widths have been cut.
If it is necessary to cut half a width, fold fabric lengthwise and cut along fold. Trim away selvedges and join width and half widths if necessary with flat fell seams. Use a loose tension and a long machine stitch for seams. A good hem is required at sides to prevent curtains from curling back. Make 1.3cm (½in) double hems at sides, tack (baste) and machine stitch or for a really good looking result stitch by hand. Turn up and hand stitch 2.5cm (1in) double hem at bottom. Turn top edge of curtain over for 6.4cm (2½in) and make a tacking (basting) line 3.8cm (1½in) down from folded edge. Cut heading tape the length required plus 5cm (2in) turning allowances. Pin and tack (baste) tape to curtain along the line of tacking (basting). Turn ends of tape under, pulling out cord from turned in ends and tack (baste) along bottom edge of tape.
Machine stitch both edges of tape to curtain. Stitch in the same direction to prevent any drag in the stitching which would show on the finished curtains.
Secure cords at ends of tape by knotting them together or stitching firmly. Draw cords up from middle of tape and ease fabric so that it is evenly gathered and the correct width for window. Knot cords in the middle and catch them to tape with one or two small stitches to prevent knot from hanging down. Gathers are easily released by cutting these stitches and undoing the knot.

Lined curtains

Professionally made lined and interlined curtains are expensive to buy, so it is a useful accomplishment to be able to make them at home. Making good curtains is not difficult, and with a little care really fine results can be achieved.

Choosing the fabric

Choose the best quality fabric you can afford for your curtains, bearing in mind the aspect of the room and the existing colour scheme. Next to the carpet, curtains give the largest amount of colour and texture to a room so it is essential that the right fabric is chosen. Remember when choosing curtain material that some fabrics drape better than others. Always ask to see the fabric draped before you buy it – it can look very different lying flat on a counter. Check, too, whether the fabric is washable or needs dry-cleaning, whether it is shrink-resistant and whether it will fade if exposed to strong sunlight.

Large abstract and geometric patterns are usually too overpowering for the average living room and if a patterned fabric is used it should be of a small design and in keeping with the size of the room. More fabric will be needed if it is patterned. A large pattern repeat can be expensive too; extra material must be allowed for matching the pattern and there is often some wastage.

Make quite sure that the pattern is printed correctly on the grain of the fabric as otherwise this can present problems when making the curtains.

Linings and interlinings
Linings

Linings are used in curtains for several reasons:

a A lining helps a curtain to drape better.

b A lining protects the curtain fabric from sun and light, and also from dust and dirt which damage the curtain fabric and make it wear out more quickly.

c A lining can act as an insulator if a metal insulated lining called Milium is used. Milium will also make a curtain draught-proof and is therefore particularly useful when used to curtain a door.

Left Nowadays, fabrics are produced to co-ordinate with wallpapers. These lined curtains use the contrast of fabric and colour most effectively, echoing the shades of the room. The tie backs look very attractive in the contrast fabric.

Above *Bathrooms have been long neglected in terms of using fabrics in an imaginative way. Here, a warmly patterned matched wallpaper and fabric have been chosen. The shower curtains should be made with a water-proof lining.*

Cotton sateen is normally used for lining curtains. This fabric is usually 122cm (48in) wide and the colours most often used are fawn and white. Although cotton sateen does come in various colours, it is desirable to line all the curtains in the house with the same colour, if possible, to give a uniform effect from the outside of the house. An exception must be made for curtains with a white background where a matching white lining is more suitable.

Interlinings

Domet, formerly used as an interlining, has largely been replaced by outing flannel or a flannel blend of cotton backed with milium. These come in white or fawn and, more rarely, gray. However, a flannelette sheet would be an acceptable substitute for either and all these materials are good insulators.

Detachable linings

It is now possible to make curtains with detachable linings if a Rufflette curtain lining tape is used. This makes it possible to wash or dry-clean the linings seperately, which is quite useful as they often seem to need cleaning before the curtains do.

When a detachable lining is used the curtains and linings are very useful in some rooms although they do not have quite the professional finish of hand made lined curtains. These have the linings stitched to the curtain round the two sides and bottom. An attached lining prevents dirt and dust from getting in between the curtain and lining fabric, giving more protection to the fabric and making it last longer.

Pelmets and valances

A valance is just like a very short curtain and is hung from a pelmet rail (rod) with curtain hooks. Valances can either be gathered or pleated as with curtain headings, so although you measure the pelmet rail (rod) in the same way as for pelmets, the measurements will be for the final gathered length. Decide on the depth you want the valance to be then calculate the amount of fabric necessary as for unlined curtains, or for pleated headings. For a uniform look match the valance to the curtains in both fabric and style and use the same type of curtain heading tape for both the curtains and the valance.

Pencil (cartridge) pleated valance

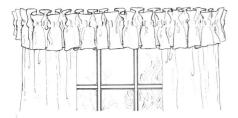

Simple gathered valance.

Figures 6 and 7 will give you ideas for styles. Make the valance as you would an unlined curtain, or if you wish to line the valance use the technique for lining pelmets.

A pelmet is a length of stiffened fabric which is hung above the curtains to conceal the curtain track and help balance the proportions of the window. It can be simply or elaborately shaped and is attached to a pelmet board, valance shelf (rod) or rail. A pelmet board should be 10.2–15.2cm (4–6in) deep and extend at least 5cm (2in) beyond each end of curtain track. Pelmets are usually tacked to pelmet boards but can also be attached with Velcro fastening. Pelmets are attached to pelmet rails with curtain hooks.

Most fabrics, unless very lightly or loosely woven, can be used for pelmets. But if curtains are very light a valance made in the same fabric, would be more suitable.

Making pattern for a pelmet

Use a sheet of brown paper sufficiently large for full length and depth of finished pelmet. Measure off length for

Left *Gingham curtains and valance*

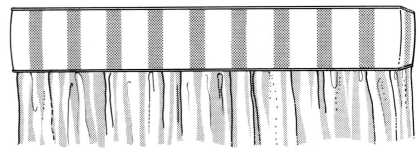

Plain and simple pelmet

Pelmet with squared ends

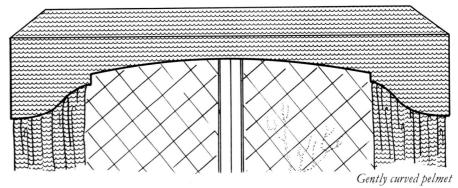

Gently curved pelmet

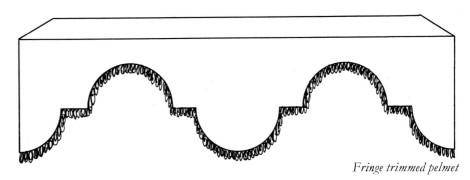

Fringe trimmed pelmet

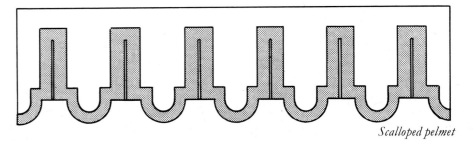

Scalloped pelmet

9

pelmet on the paper, draw in the shape you have planned to depth required (use large plate, lid or compass to help draw any curves). Fold pattern in half to check symmetry and cut out.

Making pelmet

Pin pattern to fabric, leaving 3.8cm (1½in) turning allowance. Check that any design is evenly placed before cutting out.

Cut out lining with 1.3cm (½in) turning allowance. Cut out interlining with 1.3cm (½in) turning allowance and pelmet buckram without turning allowances. Lay interlining onto wrong side of

fabric and lay buckram on interlining. Turn edges of interlining fabric over buckram, snipping into curves where necessary. The fabric should be pressed on to the pelmet buckram using a damp cloth and a hot iron.

Sew on any decorative braid or trimming before lining.

Turn under edges of lining for 1.9cm (¾in) and press.

If you are attaching pelmet to pelmet board, cut length of Velcro as long as finished pelmet. Stitch one half along top edge of turned-in lining on the right side. Lay lining on pelmet, wrong sides facing,

Above *Covered pelmet in matching fabric with curtains and bedspreads.*

and hem in place around edges. Stick other half of Velcro along pelmet board, flush with top edge, using very strong adhesive. When dry, pelmet is simply pressed in place.

The pelmet should be fixed to the board by using a strong tape sewn to the back of the pelmet and pockets should be made so that drawing pins can be used.

For a pelmet rail (rod) Insert the hooks into the heading tape and hang the pelmet as if it were an ungathered curtain.

Curtain headings

There are several types of attractive headings which can be made to give curtains an elegant finish, without using pelmets. The simplest to make is a standard gathered heading, which takes the least amount of fabric and is suitable for all weights of material.

Pencil (cartridge) pleated headings take rather more fabric and are particularly suitable for heavier fabrics which need to fall in generous but well regulated folds. For a really elegant heading, pinch pleats display satins, velvets and large prints to their fullest advantage.

Measuring for curtains

Measure the length of the curtain rail (rod), or the combined length of both rails (rods) where two overlap. More often than not this will be wider than the window itself. Measure the overall curtain length from the height of the heading required, adding an extra 20.3cm (8in) for hems and headings.

Patterned curtains will need extra fabric so that the pattern runs on the same level on all curtains and an allowance for shrinkage should be made when buying all curtain and lining fabrics. Check with the retailer for details.

Full length curtains should finish 2.5cm (1in) above the floor to allow them to hang properly and to protect the fabric from wear. Similarly, shorter curtains should either fall just above the window sill, or just below it.

Stitching the tape

If the curtain rail (rod) is fixed to the wall, with plenty of space above it, stitch the tape with the hook pockets at the bottom. Where the curtains are suspended below the rail (rod), such as on a decorative pole or from a rail fixed to the ceiling, stitch the tape with the hook pockets at the top.

Standard gathered headings

Curtain fabric (standard headings)

The fabric required to make the curtains must be at least 1½ times the width of the curtain rail (rod), including any overlap, plus an allowance of 7.6cm (3in) for the side hems and 3.2cm (1¼in) for each seam. Using Standard Rufflette tape, 2.5cm (1in) wide, you will need the same amount of tape as the curtain fabric width.

Join the curtain widths where necessary taking a 1.6cm (⅝in) seam allowance. Make side hems on the curtains taking an allowance of 3.8cm (1½in) each.

Pin and tack (baste) a 3.8cm (1½in) turning along the top edge of the curtains.

Pencil (cartridge) pleated net curtains

Preparing the tape

Pull out approximately 3.8cm (1½in) of each cord at one end of the tape, and knot them together.

Trim off the surplus tape.

Turn this prepared end under so that the knotted ends are enclosed (fig. 1).

At the other end of the tape, pull out the same amount of cord and leave the ends free for pleating.

Turn under the end of the tape to make a neat finish. The knotted end of the tape should always be stitched to the edge of the curtain which is at the centre of the rail, the loose cords can be suspended from the outside edge.

Making sure that the hook pockets are facing outwards, pin and tack (baste) the tape in position on the curtain so that it covers the raw edge of the turning, and is 2.5cm (1in) in from the top edge (fig. 2). Stitch all around the outer edge of the tape keeping the stitching line outside the cords and as close as possible to the edge of the tape. It is advisable to machine stitch in the same direction along the top and bottom of the tape to avoid causing any drag in the stitching.

Pleating the curtains

Holding one end of the tape firmly, pull the fabric along the cords until all the fabric is packed to one end of the tape. Gently pull the fabric out again to the required width and knot the cords tightly to hold the heading in place. Insert curtain hooks at each end of the tape, and at 7.6cm (3in) intervals along the length of the curtains.

Do not cut off the surplus cord as this allows the curtains to be pulled flat for washing and ironing.

When the curtains have been pleated, wind the surplus cord around the fingers into a neat coil.

Secure with thread and suspend neatly out of sight at the outer edges of the curtains. Having tried the curtains for length, tack (baste) and stitch a temporary hem, which may need altering after cleaning or washing.

Pencil (cartridge) pleated headings

The amount of fabric required for pencil (cartridge) pleating must be 2½ times the width of the curtain rail (rod), plus any overlap.

Make up the curtains as for a standard gathered heading, but make a 1.6cm (⅝in) turning along the top edge.

Prepare the tape in the same way as before, using tape especially for this.

Making sure the hook pockets are facing outward and the knotted end of the tape is to the centre of the curtain, tack the tape to the centre of the curtain, so that the edges meet along the top.

Stitch all round the edge of the tape, keeping the stitching outside the cords and as close to the edge as possible.

Pinch pleated headings

There are two versions of this type of tape, for curtains which conceal the rail (rod) and for curtains which are suspended below it. There is also a version for smaller windows and light-

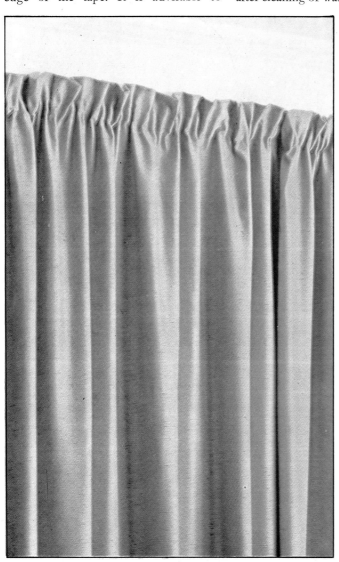

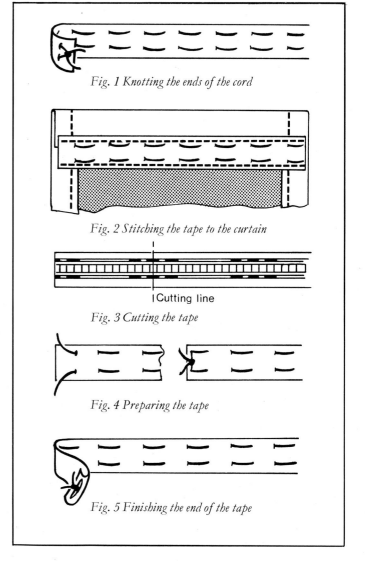

Fig. 1 Knotting the ends of the cord

Fig. 2 Stitching the tape to the curtain

Cutting line

Fig. 3 Cutting the tape

Fig. 4 Preparing the tape

Fig. 5 Finishing the end of the tape

weight fabrics. So buy the appropriate type of tape required.

The fabric needed for pinch pleating must be at least twice the width of the curtain rail (rod), plus the usual allowances.

You will need the same length of tape as the width of fabric required.

Make up the curtains in the usual way, and pin and tack (baste) a 1.6cm ($\frac{5}{8}$in) turning along the top edge of the curtain. Making sure the tape is the right way up, make a cut in the centre of the first group of pleats (fig. 3).

Pull out the ends of the cord and knot them together. Trim off the surplus tape 1.3cm ($\frac{1}{2}$in) from the cord (fig. 4).

Turn under 2.5cm (1in) at the end of the tape, including the knotted ends of the cord (fig. 5). Lay the tape over the top of the curtain with the folded end level with the centre edge of the curtain and the top edge close to the top of the curtain.

Stitch across the folded edge and along the top edge of the tape.

If the tape ends at a space at the side of the curtain, use the point of a pair of scissors to pick out the cords, and trim the tape to within 1.3cm ($\frac{1}{2}$in) of the cord. Making sure that the ends of the cord the tape and stitch along this edge, but not over the cords. Stitch along the bottom edge of the tape a little way in from the edge.

To pleat the curtains

Hold the free ends of the cord firmly, and push the first set of pleats into position along the cords. The spaces between the pleats must be kept flat and unpuckered. Push the second set of pleats into pos-ition and then push the first set into position again.

Proceed in this way until all the pleats are in position along the heading. Try the curtain on the rail (rod) and adjust the pleats if necessary so that they fit exactly.

Above *Pencil (cartridge) pleated headings fall gracefully into long folds. Here the curtains are hung from the ceiling to the floor – an excellent way of creating a sense of height in a room.*

Opposite *A detail of curtains with pinch pleated headings. They are made by attaching special tape, and the diagrams show how it is prepared and attached.*

Linings and interlinings

Detachable linings can be made if desired and attached to the curtains by the same hooks which suspend the curtain from the rail (rod).

You will need 1½ to twice the width of the curtain rail (rod) in lining fabric, plus the usual allowances.

Make up as for the curtains, using lining (drapery) tape, and pleat to match

Below A cosy, cottage-style fabric with a pretty pink and blue floral pattern is used to make these delightful curtains. The matching valance has a delicately pleated heading.

the curtain width.

Tapes and hooks

Here are some of the most widely used heading tapes:

Standard heading tape: this is a 2.5cm (1in) wide tape for even gathering on all types of fabrics where a simple gathered heading is required. The tape comes in a variety of colours and has two cords for drawing up the fullness.

Kirsch Easypleat, and similar deep pleating tapes: these are for making pinch pleats easily. No cord is used for drawing up the tapes, but special deep pleat hooks are required and the pleated effect is achieved by inserting the prongs of the hooks in the pockets on the tape. Single, double or triple pleats can be made. When using the tapes it is necessary to work out carefully the quantity of fabric required and the number of sets of pleats in each curtain. Some companies produce a tape and fabric calculator for this purpose.

Rufflette Regis and special tape: for making pencil (cartridge) pleats. No special hook is required for this tape; the standard plastic hook is used. The tape is made of nylon and is hard wearing and strong, standing up well to washing and dry-cleaning. Two cords are used to draw up the tape and so form the pleats. There are other ways of making pencil (cartridge) pleats and special hooks are used. Various detailed leaflets are available on these and other heading styles and can be obtained from most soft furnishing counters.

Curtain tracks
Choice of heading

There are so many different types of curtain track and heading tape available that it is advisable to give your curtain headings some thought and to decide on the effect required. Decorative curtain poles are very much in fashion again and can look most attractive used with pleated or deeply gathered heading tapes. Many different effects can be achieved by using the new tracks and headings and it is advisable to find a soft furnishing or hardware store which displays some of them.

If a lined or interlined curtain is being used, make sure when choosing a track that it is strong enough to take the weight. Curtain tracks these days are made for use with or without pelmets and with conventional or deep headings. Some tracks can be bent to fit around curves;

some are made in plastic or nylon, others are made from metal or wood. Some have a perfectly plain 'front', others have a decorative finish.

When you choose a track you should first consider the type in relation to the shape of the window, then to the room, its other furnishings and the style and weight of the curtains. It is always worth actually selecting the track in a store which has a large number of different types displayed so you can compare them and examine the fittings (you can always buy it locally, if that is more convenient). Many shops also show tracks complete with curtains so you can judge them for smooth running and noise.

Choosing for the window

If your windows are straight, with a few inches of wall above, almost all types of track are suitable. You simply have to decide on the best style. With bay and some dormer windows, however, the choice is more limited.

Where the bay is either square or angled, it may be possible to fit a separate track to each section. This means that on the most common style of bay, which is made up of three sections, you would need a minimum of four curtains – a pair for the centre section and one for each side. This works quite well, although it can be a little inconvenient and also reduces the amount of daylight allowed into the room when the curtains are open.

The alternative – and the only style possible on a circular bay – is to use a track which can be bent to the right shape. There are some tracks which you buy in a straight piece and bend it yourself, that your local dealer can suggest. Or for heavy curtains you can have the track custom-made.

On some dormer windows, if you fit a straight track, the curtains may block out too much light when they are open. Here it may be a good idea, if the walls at each side of the window are deep enough, to buy a track 15.2cm (6in) longer than the width of the window and bend it 7.6cm (3in) at each end around into the room. Then the curtains can be pulled right around to hang against the wall at each side.

It is usually best to hang curtains outside a window reveal, but often this is not practical – in a bathroom or kitchen, for example. So that the curtains do not have to rub against the window (which they might with a track fixed to the wall above

Right *Nowadays, poles (rods) are very fashionable for hanging curtains.*

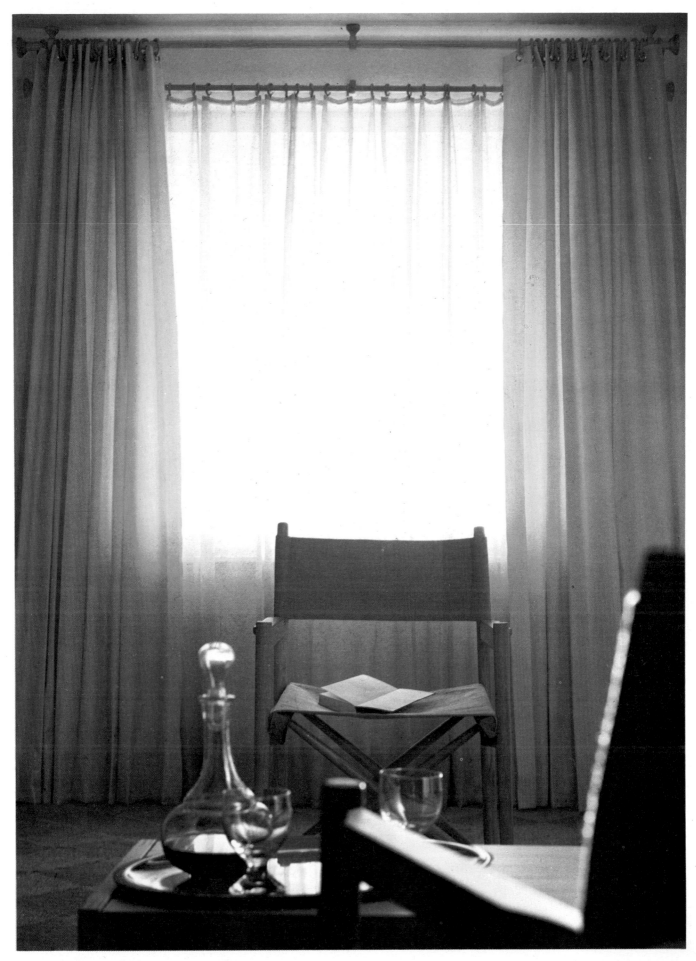

it), it may be better to use an unobtrusive track, which can be fixed to the ceiling of the reveal (soffit).

Choosing for the room

In choosing the style of curtains, one of the main decisions is whether or not to have a pelmet. If you have decided against one, you are then plunged into the next decision: the style of curtain track.

The standard type of metal track which was the only sort available for many years, is considered by many people to be too ugly for use without a pelmet. The 'works' of the runners are visible from the front, and on most windows two sections of track are needed so that the curtains can overlap in the middle when they are drawn. Other disadvantages are that it collects dust and is noisy in use, although application of a little silicone wax helps this.

The nylon equivalent of this type is much quieter and easier to clean, and is often used for curtains with a plain heading where there is no pelmet. Its other advantages are that it is cheap and is easily bent to fit bays.

For a more streamlined effect, a plain strip, where the mechanics of the runner are hidden behind, is very popular. There are several different makes, all very similar. Some versions, however, look best with curtains which have deep headings, because plain headings tend to drop or fall back.

With this type of track, only one length is needed on straight runs because there is a special fitting which can be used on one of the curtains so that it will overlap the other when closed.

The overlap fitting is about 5–7.6cm (2–3in) long and slots on the track in the same way as the runners. It normally has two or three holes into which the hooks at the end of the curtain can be fitted, and it moves along the track with the curtain. Because the arm is curved to come out about 1.3cm ($\frac{1}{2}$in) from the track, the edge of the other curtain can fit in behind it when the curtains are closed. When the curtains are open, the arm is not noticeable at all, but the curtain to which it is attached does not pull back quite as far as the other one.

Another point about this fitting, which might be a drawback in some cases, is that the curtain it is attached to has to be about 10.2cm (4in) wider than the other one after the gathers are pulled up. If possible, you should allow for this in the initial cutting out of the curtains. Where doing this would upset the balance of the fabric's pattern, it might be better to make both curtains the same size before gathering, and to settle for the overlapping ones being slightly less tightly pleated.

Left *These dramatically patterned curtains, splashed with a large art nouveau type flower motif are hung from a carved wooden track which enhances the design.*

If you want the effect of the plain band, but also want to fit it around a bay, an aluminium track, may be a better choice. This track can be bent to a curve (not a sharp angle) with a 12.7cm (5in) radius without affecting its performance or breaking. It has a combined glide hook which is clipped on to the track from the front. The prong of the hook can be inserted into the pockets of the gathering tape, thus holding a plain heading upright. For a deep heading, separate hooks can be used and hung from the ring at the base of the glide.

Most plain tracks are designed so that they are concealed by the curtains when closed, but if you have one of the decorative types you can sew on deep heading tape so that the pockets come at the top in order to reveal the track when the curtains are closed.

At the opposite end of the scale for straight runs, there are the decorative curtain poles. Curtain poles were the original way of hanging curtains with rings which were attached to the curtain and slid along the pole. They did not run very smoothly or quietly, and because the rings were sewn to the curtains these had to be removed each time the curtains were cleaned, and then sewn on again.

Nowadays this method has been modified to give the same effect, but the curtains run more smoothly because the rings, which encircle the pole, have much smaller rings at their base into which the curtain hooks can be slotted. In other versions no large rings are used, but small ones glide along a groove at the base of the pole. With most poles it is possible to fit an overlap arm and a cording set.

The poles are made in different finishes – brass, aluminium or wood painted in different colours – so you can choose the best one for your room. They also have a variety of end pieces which can be screwed into place.

All these poles look best with curtains with a deep heading – pinch pleats especially – and they also need a fairly 'grand' setting. They are more expensive than most other kinds of curtain track, but some have the advantage of being expandable so if you move you can normally adjust the pole to fit another window.

Choosing for the curtains

If you are having a pelmet or valance, the best sort of track to use is the standard metal kind, or its slightly less strong nylon equivalent. It is the least expensive type of track to buy, it is easy to fit, can be bent easily, and all the mechanics are hidden by the pelmet.

If you are having a gathered valance, you can combine it with a valance rail (rod). The curtain track is fixed in the usual way and the valance rail (rod) is clipped onto it by a nylon bracket so that it stands away from the track to allow easy movement in closing the curtains.

If you also want net curtains with this type of track, it is possible to use a bracket which holds both tracks about 2.5–5cm (1–2in) apart. Alternatively, for straight runs, you can buy a special top fixed combined track which has two channels.

If you are not using a pelmet but have curtains with a plain gathered heading, the best sort of track to use is one with a combination glide hook (see above), because this prevents the heading from falling back, and when the curtains are closed the track is completely covered.

Most kinds of track can be used with a deep heading, providing there is enough clearance above the track – a minimum of 6mm ($\frac{1}{4}$in) – to allow the curtain to move freely along. With decorative poles, however, this is not a problem because they are designed to allow the pole to be visible when the curtains are closed.

Whichever sort of track is used, it is essential to check that it will be strong enough for the weight of the curtains. With most fabrics there is no need to worry, as long as the track has been fixed securely. But on full length, lined and interlined velvet curtains, for example, a lightweight plastic or aluminium track is not strong enough and you should use a heavy-duty metal track.

Measuring for the track

In order to allow as much light as possible to come into the room when the curtains are open, it is usually better to hang curtains outside a window reveal, rather than immediately next to the window. Unless you want to use the curtains to camouflage the shape of the window, the track should be long enough to extend about 15.2cm (6in) on each side of the reveal so that the curtains can be pulled right back. On extra wide windows, or when the curtains are very bulky, you may want to make the track even longer.

If you are limited in space, and are using a decorative pole, remember that the end pieces may add about 5–7.6cm (2–3in) on each end but without actually increasing the length of the usable track. With some other tracks, adding a cording set may make a difference to the length of track you buy, because the fittings can add some extra width at each side.

Most tracks are sold in set lengths, increasing at 15.2cm (6in) or 30.5cm (1ft) intervals. You simply buy the length nearest your own, and cut it to the right size if necessary. Some other types are expandable and simply need adjusting to size.

Before you buy the track, decide on whether you are going to fix it to the ceiling or the wall above the window. Fixing it to the wall is more satisfactory in most cases, but where there is no room above the window or where the curtains are to come within a reveal, it may be preferable to fix it to the ceiling. Some tracks are supplied with brackets which can be used either way, but with others you may have to buy a special bracket.

Fitting a cording set may seem like an extravagance, but in fact they are well worth the money. Most tracks work better with one, and there is less strain put on them. They also save the edges of the curtains from soiling and wearing out through constant handling.

Some more expensive tracks are supplied already fitted with a cording set. With others you buy a kit, complete with cord, pulleys and weights, and fit it to the track yourself.

Fixing the track

Most tracks are supplied with instructions and all the necessary brackets and screws for fixing it into position. If you are securing the track to a wall, it is essential that the holes for the screws are correctly and adequately plugged and for heavy curtains it is more than likely that the screws supplied by the manufacturer will not be long enough.

One of the simplest methods of fixing the brackets for a straight run is to screw them to a wooden batten 5cm x 2.5cm (2in x 1in), which can then be screwed to the wall. In this way, you can ensure that all the brackets are level, which is never easy if you are drilling several holes into the wall, and you can use the edge of the batten to mark the fixing line.

Using a batten is also a neat way of bringing the track away from the wall enough to allow the curtains to clear the window sill. Alternatively, you can use special extension brackets which are made to go with most tracks.

If you are bending the track for a bay window, be careful to make smooth curves, not angles, or the curtains will not run smoothly.

Sheer curtains

Sheer curtains add charm and can also make an attractive screen in a dining alcove.

The fabric

Sheer curtain fabrics fall into two categories: fine nets and semi-sheers.

Fine nets are the traditional type, hung against the window to give privacy to a room which can be seen into. The fabric used to be cotton, but these days it is more often a man-made fibre such as Terylene (Dacron) which is strong and resistant to the sun. Fine net curtains are normally white and are combined with heavier main curtains which give complete screening at night.

Semi-sheers, such as those shown in the photograph, are heavier than fine nets and have a more open weave. They look particularly attractive with large modern windows where they diffuse the light rather than obscure it. They can also make attractive room dividers.

Semi-sheers are made in a variety of colours, weaves and textures, mostly from acrylic fibres which give a warm feel. The curtains are decorative and heavy enough to be hung outside the window recess, and main curtains are not often necessary. For complete screening at night, however, you could make a detachable lining to hang from the same track as the sheers so that the lining is pulled across at the same time. If you wish, they can be removed in summer. Or, if you like to leave the curtains drawn across the window during the day, the lining could be made to hang from a separate track next to the window and be drawn at night.

The amount of fabric

Both types of sheer curtains are measured and made up in a similar way to unlined curtains. The main difference is that they should be much fuller – up to three times the width of the area they are to cover.

To save joining several lengths together, which can look ugly as the seams show through to the right side, it is normally better to make several curtains, each of a fabric width, instead of the traditional pair. When these are hung, the edges are hidden by the folds and the effect is one of a complete curtain.

Fortunately semi-sheer curtain fabrics are often made in extra wide widths – sometimes twice the normal 122cm (48in). With fine nets you can often buy the fabric in a set length nearest to the one you require, and the width required is measured off the roll in the same way as the length is measured off for regular fabrics. The hem and heading are already made and you simply have to finish the side hems.

Sewing sheer curtains

Sheer fabrics are not difficult to sew provided you use a fine sharp needle and set your machine with a loose tension to prevent puckering. It is always advisable to tack (baste) all folds, hems and seams as the fabric tends to slip while it is being machine stitched. You should also use synthetic thread and gathering tape as this will behave in the same way as the fabric.

If you have difficulty in feeding the fabric through the machine or if it still slips in spite of being tacked (basted), it may help to put strips of tissue paper under the fabric as it is being fed into the machine. This can be torn away afterward.

Another important point in making sheer curtains of both types is that all the hems – side, bottom and top – must be made double with equal first and second turnings, so you will not get an ugly raw edge showing through to the right side of the curtain. With semi-sheers, you should also plan the width of the hems and turnings so that the spaces in the weave of the fabric fall on top of each other and the stitching can be worked on a solid section of the weave. In many cases you may not have to make side hems as the selvedges make perfectly good edges.

Deep headings

Because of their additional fullness, both types of sheer curtains can be made with a deep heading tape giving either pencil (cartridge) or pinch pleats.

These are available in a man-made fibre and are stitched on in a similar way to the narrower standard tape. The essential difference is that the top edge of the curtain should be turned over for the exact depth of the tape and the top edge of the tape should be placed just below the fold.

If you do not like the effect of the curtain tape showing through the mesh of semi-sheers, you can disguise it by inserting a strip of plain fabric in a colour to match the curtains between the curtain and the tape. The strip should be of a similar fibre to the curtains so that it will react in the same way when washed. Alternatively you could stitch a decorative braid of the same width as the tape on to the front of the curtains.

See through curtains

In a fine cotton lawn with a broderie frill these enchanting curtains are a cool cover-up for any room in the house. And they are easy enough for beginners.

The curtains

They are made from white lawn and have a gathered broderie anglaise frill along the hem and front edge, with another frill below the casing at the top. The curtains are hung on expanding wire which hooks on to the window frame, and are tied back during the day with frilled bands.

How much fabric to buy
1 First measure for the width of the

fabric needed in each of the two curtains, simply by measuring the width of the window. By allowing this full width in each curtain, which covers half the width of window, you will have a pleasing double fullness.

It is normally simplest to work in full or half widths of fabric and the width of the curtains can be adjusted to suit this if necessary, but there should never be less than a fullness-and-a-half.

2 Next, measure for the length, from the top of the window to the window sill. From this, subtract the depth of the frill and multiply the final amount by the number of widths required for both curtains. Allow 1.37m ($1\frac{1}{2}$yd) extra for the turnings and tie backs.

3 The gathered frills are made from broderie anglaise trimming 15.2cm (6in) or 20.3cm (8in) wide, of the type sold by the yard. Alternatively you could use broderie anglaise fabric and trim off the required depth for the edging.

In either case for the trimming, you will need to buy an amount equal to: 6 times the width of the curtains plus 3 times the length plus about 2.30m ($2\frac{1}{2}$yd) for the two tie backs.

Making the curtains

1 Cut out two pieces of lawn to the measurements calculated above, but 1.9cm ($\frac{3}{4}$in) shorter (because the casing is added separately).

2 To make the left-hand curtain of the pair, start by stitching a 2.5cm (1in) hem along the left-hand edge. To do this, turn under 6mm ($\frac{1}{4}$in) on to the wrong side and press down. Turn the edge over for another 2.5cm (1in), tack (baste) and machine stitch. Press again.

3 Turn up a 6mm ($\frac{1}{4}$in) fold onto the right side along the bottom and right-hand edge. Press and tack (baste).

4 Cut off a length of trimming equal to $1\frac{1}{2}$ times the combined width and length of the curtain, plus 3.8cm ($1\frac{1}{2}$in) for turnings.

5 To prepare the trimming make a small hem along the bottom edge if you are using broderie anglaise fabric. On all trimmings, turn under 1.3cm ($\frac{1}{2}$in) onto the wrong side along the left-hand short edge. Turn over 2.5cm (1in) more, tack (baste) and machine stitch. Leave the right-hand short edge raw.

Turn 1cm ($\frac{3}{8}$in) onto the wrong side along the top edge, tack (baste) and press.

6 Make two rows of gathering stitches (like running stitch if you are doing it by hand, or with a long machine stitch), one 6mm ($\frac{1}{4}$in) below this.

7 Draw up the gathering threads so that the frill fits the bottom and right-hand side of the curtain. Lay out the curtain with the right side facing up and the bottom edge toward you. Place on the trimming, with the wrong side facing down with its top edge 1.3cm ($\frac{1}{2}$in) above the bottom edge of the curtain. Distribute the gathers evenly, allowing more at the corner so that the frill will hang well. The raw edge of the frill should be level with the raw edge at the top of the curtain. Pin and tack (baste) in position.

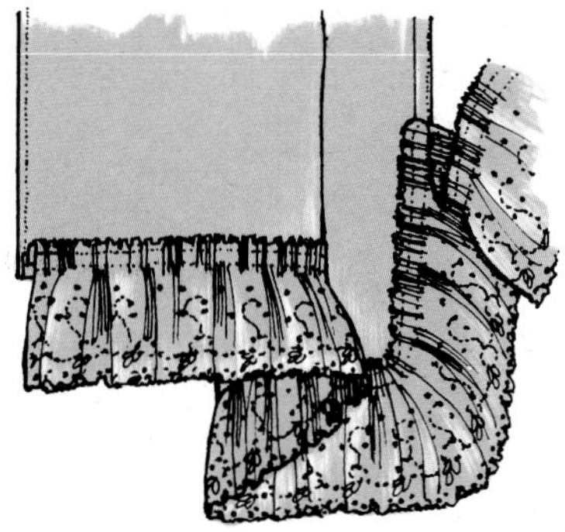

8 Stitch with two lines of machine stitches just above the gathering lines.

9 Measure the width of the curtain, including the frill, and cut a 10.1cm (4in) wide strip of lawn to this length, plus 2.5cm (1in) for the casing.

Fold under each short end of the strip for 6mm ($\frac{1}{4}$in) on the wrong side and press. Fold over another 6mm ($\frac{1}{4}$in) and tack (baste) and machine stitch. Fold the strip in half lengthwise with the wrong side inside, and work a line of machining 20.3cm (8in) from the folded edge.

10 Place the strip on the wrong side at the top of the curtain with the raw edges level, and machine stitch through the three thicknesses, 6mm ($\frac{1}{4}$in) from the edge. Press the turnings onto the curtain.

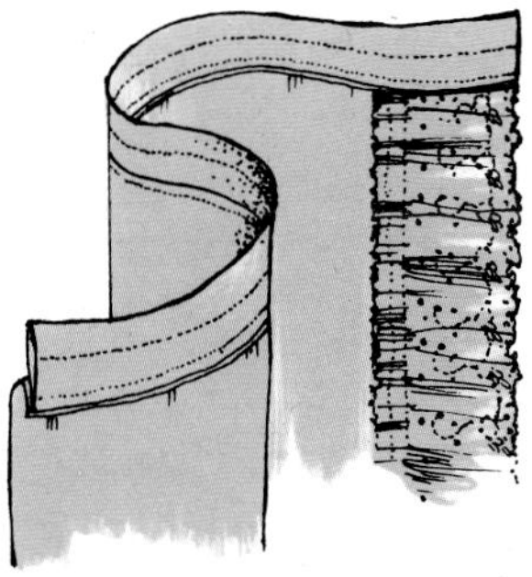

11 Cut a length of trimming equal to $1\frac{1}{2}$ times the total width of the curtain, plus 7.6cm (3in) and prepare it as before but making hems along both short edges.

12 Place it on the right side of the curtain so that its top edge is 6mm ($\frac{1}{4}$in) above the seam line of the casing. Machine stitch along this line and 6mm ($\frac{1}{4}$in) below, so that the raw edges of the seam are enclosed.

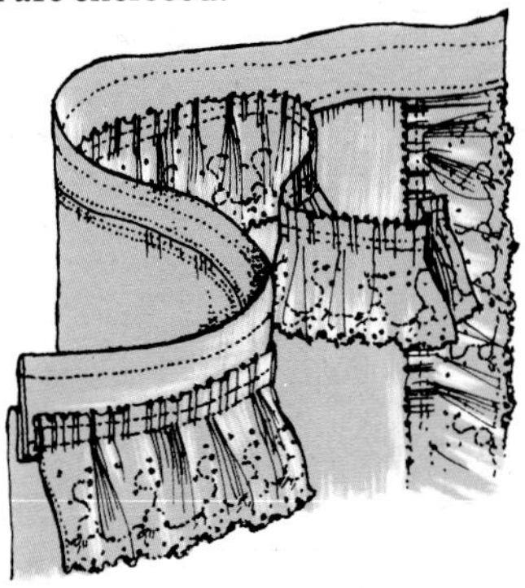

13 Make the right-hand curtain in a similar way, but reverse the instructions so that the frill is attached along the left-hand edge and bottom.

Tie backs

1 Cut two strips of lawn, 45.5cm x 7.5cm (18in x 3in). Make hems along the short edges as before, then make one along one of the long edges. Turn up a 6mm ($\frac{1}{4}$in) fold on to the right side along the remaining edge.

2 Cut a 91.5cm (36in) length of trimming, make hems at each end and gather the top edge as before. Place it over the raw edge of the strip and stitch in position.

3 Sew on 6mm ($\frac{1}{2}$in) diameter curtain rings at both ends of the strip, so that the tie backs can be hooked onto small hooks screwed into the wall at the side of the curtains.

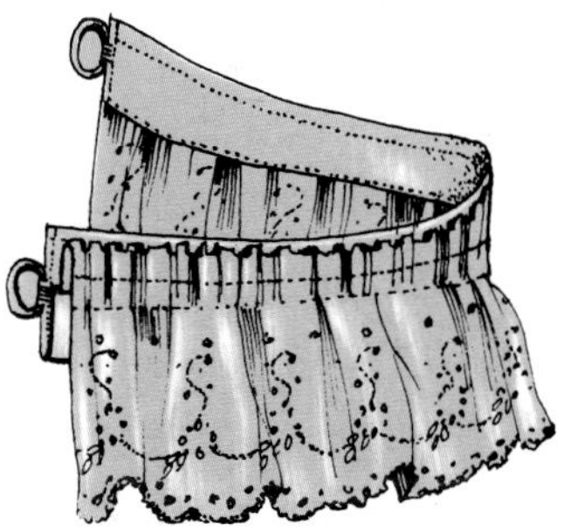

Hanging the curtains

Place the curtains so that the frilled sides are in the middle. Slot the expanding wire through the casing formed between the machine stitched line and the top of the frill of both curtains. Try the curtains in position against the window and screw the side hooks to the window frame at the correct height. Arrange the gathers evenly on the wire and add the tie backs.

Unlined curtains

Unlined curtains are simple and quick to make and are ideal in a room like the kitchen where they may need frequent washing. Make them in a gaily patterned cotton, towelling or lightweight man-made fibre.

The amount of fabric
This is calculated by measuring the width and height of the window area. If the curtains hang outside the window recess, take the measurements from the track from which they will hang as this probably extends some way on each side of the recess and is fixed a little above it.

Measuring the width
Ideally each curtain should be cut double the width of the area it is to cover so that when it is gathered it will have a pleasing fullness. Usually, however, it is simpler to base the width on full and half widths of fabric so there is no wastage. The small difference this makes can be adjusted in the gathering.
1 Measure the length of the curtain track with a wood or steel rule. Add 10.2cm (4in) and divide the width of the fabric into the total, rounding it off up or down to the nearest half width.
2 This gives the number of widths required in each curtain, so double it to give the number of widths for a pair of curtains.

Measuring the length
Curtains hung inside the window recess should finish at the sill, or if they are hung outside the recess, 7.6cm–10.2cm (3–4in) below the sill.
1 Measure from the top of the track to the required length and add 15.2cm (6in) for a double hem at the foot and 3.8cm ($1\frac{1}{2}$in) for the heading.
2 Multiply this figure by the total number of widths to give the minimum amount of fabric required for the curtains.
3 If the fabric is patterned you will have to buy extra so that it can be matched on all the widths. Check on the size of the pattern repeat and as a guide allow one extra on each width. For example, if each curtain is made from two widths, you should allow four extra pattern repeats for a pair of curtains.

Left *A small kitchen window is brought into focus by matching the curtain fabric with the wallpaper design.*

4 If the fabric is not guaranteed non-shrink, allow an extra 2.5cm per 91.4cm (1in per square yard), and wash the fabric before cutting out.

Gathering tape
The easiest way of gathering the curtains is to stitch on tape which has cords along each edge which can be drawn up, and pockets for the curtain hooks to be inserted.
For unlined curtains, use tape which is 2.5cm (1in) wide. This is available in a variety of colours, in cotton for natural fibres and nylon for man-made fibres. Buy a piece equal to the width of each curtain, plus 5.1cm (2in) for turnings.

Cutting out
1 Iron the fabric to remove all the creases and lay it out, right side up, on a large flat surface. You must be able to see a complete curtain length at once, so use the floor if you do not have a table large enough.
2 Make the top edge square with the selvedges by pulling out a thread across the width. Cut along this line. Measure the total length of the curtain from this point, withdraw another thread and cut along it.
3 Place the top edge of the cut length alongside the next length so you can see how the pattern matches, adjust it if necessary and trim off any wastage from the top edge. Cut the next length in the same way. For a half width, fold the length in half and cut down the fold.

cutting line

Joining the widths
1 For plain fabrics, pin the pieces together with right sides facing and selvedges matching. Place half widths on the outside edge of each curtain.
2 Tack (baste) and machine stitch, taking 1.3cm ($\frac{1}{2}$in) turnings. Trim one side of the turnings to 6mm ($\frac{1}{4}$in) and press both turnings to one side so that the un-

23

trimmed one is on top. Fold under the edge of this one 6mm ($\frac{1}{4}$in) and slip-stitch to complete a fell seam.

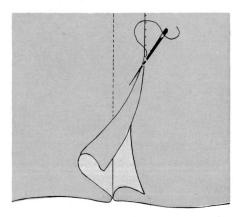

3 To join patterned fabrics, press the turnings under for 1.3cm ($\frac{1}{2}$in), or the width of the selvedge if this is more, on one of the pieces. Place the fold over the edge of the other piece so that the pattern matches.

4 Pin the pieces together from the front and slip tack (baste) in place. To do this, insert the needle into the fold on the first width and withdraw it 6mm ($\frac{1}{4}$in) further on. Take it directly across to the second width and insert it. Pass it under the fabric and withdraw 6mm ($\frac{1}{4}$in) further on. Continue like this for the length of the curtains. You will then find you can stitch the pieces together on the wrong side in the normal way. Complete the join with a fell seam as for plain fabrics.

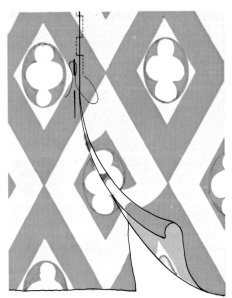

The side hems

1 Make 2.5cm (1in) double hems along the sides of the curtain as these are heavier than normal hems and prevent the sides from curling back. To make the hems, fold over the edges for 2.5cm

(1in) on the wrong side of the fabric. Press.

2 Fold over the edges for a further 2.5cm (1in), tack (baste) and slip stitch or machine stitch in position. Press.

Attaching the tape

1 Fold over the raw edge at the top of each curtain for 3.8cm (1$\frac{1}{2}$in) on the wrong side and press down.

2 Cut a length of tape the width of the curtain, plus 5.1cm (2in). Pull out about 2.5cm (1in) of the cords from their slots at each end of the tape. Knot the cords together at one end but leave their other ends free for gathering.

3 Place the tape on the wrong side of the curtain so that it covers the raw edge of the turning centrally, and the top edge of the tape is 2.5cm (1in) from the top of the curtain.

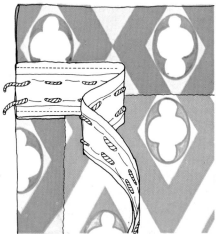

4 Turn under the short ends of the tape, enclosing the knotted cords at one end but leaving them free at the other end. Tack (baste) it to the curtain all around the edge.

5 Machine stitch outside the cords on each side, stitching in the same direction on the top and bottom to prevent dragging.

Gathering the curtains

1 Pull the curtain along the cords until it is gathered tightly at the knotted end. Pull out to the correct width, distributing the gathers evenly.

2 Knot the cords to secure the width but do not cut off the surplus ends. These can be wound up and caught to the tape with a few stitches and can be unpicked to release the cords when you wash the curtains.

3 Insert curtain hooks at ends of each curtain and at 7.6cm (3in) intervals between. Hang the curtains for a few

days before taking up the bottom hems as the fabric may drop a little.

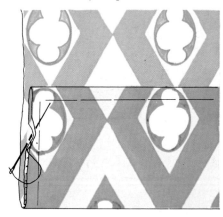

Making the hems

1 Mark the required length of the curtain with pins across the width while they are still hanging. Take them down, check that the line is level and that the sides are the same length and correct if necessary.

2 Turn up the hem along the marked line and tack (baste) loosely along it. Turn under the raw edge for half the total depth of the hem allowance and tack (baste). Slip stitch along this fold and down the sides of the hems.

3 Press the hem, remove all tacking (basting and re-hang the finished curtains.

Café Curtains

Café curtains originated in France in the old coffee houses and are still to be seen in restaurant windows in many parts of Europe. They usually cover only the lower part of the window, and are used when privacy is required without blocking out daylight. Café curtains are hung in various ways: sometimes they are simply hung on a rod; or they can be gathered on tape for different effects; or can be made with cut-out headings and suspended from hooks or rings. So café curtains are not only functional, they can be decorative too, and make a striking change from the traditional half window nets. Trimmed with braid or matched to roller blinds or pelmets, they are particularly effective in rooms where the windows are extra large and where traditional curtains would be very expensive.

It is worth remembering that café curtains will allow the maximum amount of light into a room; light coming from nearer the ceiling is more valuable than light coming in at a lower level.

Measuring for café curtains

To measure for café curtains first decide on the 'drop' required. This is the finished length of the curtain. It will probably be determined by the amount of privacy needed, but café curtains usually cover half the window. Sometimes two curtains are used, one for the top half of the window and one for the bottom half. These are called 'tiered cafés' and are both made in exactly the same way.

Café curtains usually hang either to the sill or 5.1–10.2cm (2–4in) below the sill. Sometimes they hang to the floor, perhaps to cover a radiator, but they should never fall in between unless a window seat or other piece of furniture has to be cleared or they will look out of proportion to the window.

Measure the track with a yardstick or steel rule, not a tape measure as these tend to stretch and an accurate measurement cannot be obtained. Allow $1\frac{1}{2}$ times the length of the track if a lined curtain with a scalloped heading is being used. $1\frac{1}{2}$ to $2\frac{1}{2}$ times the length of the track will be necessary if the curtain is unlined or a fancy heading tape is being used. The width needed depends on the

Above *Café curtains are becoming very popular in the modern home. The ones illustrated are beautifully made with scalloped headings, and are hung on an attractive pole (rod).*

weight and texture of the fabric – lighter, more delicate fabrics look better with extra fullness.

Allow 15.2cm (6in) for turnings (i.e. for top and bottom hems), if using a standard or deep heading tape. For scalloped headings more allowance is necessary for the scallop. Allow extra material if using a patterned fabric and work out the repeats to see if the curtain lengths will cut economically. Remember when choosing the fabric to ask the size of the pattern repeat as large repeats can be expensive.

Linings

It is not usually necessary to line café curtains. If they are unlined the maximum of light will filter through. However, some fabrics may look more effective used with a light cotton lining and less fullness, particularly where a pattern can be shown to advantage.

Tracks and headings

Decorative brass poles or wooden or plastic rods can be used for hanging café curtains in exactly the same way as traditional curtains. Brass or plastic or wooden rings can be sewn to the top of the curtain or clip-on rings can be used.

Scalloped café curtains

These instructions are for unlined café curtains.

Fabric requirements

To calculate the length decide on the drop of the curtain. Also decide on the depth of the scallop required and add this measurement plus 12.7cm (5in) for turnings to the curtain length.

Allow 1½ times the measurement of the track for the width of the curtain depending on the fabric used. In the case of a scalloped heading less fullness may be necessary to show up the shaped top to advantage. Sheer material is not usually suitable for scalloped headings for this reason.

Sides and hems

First cut off the selvedges to avoid pulling, and fold and tack (baste) 1.2cm (½in) double hems at both sides of the curtain. Turn up the bottom hem 5.1cm (2in) and make a 2.5cm (1in) double hem.

Hand or machine stitch side and bottom hems. Hand stitched hems look better and hang well, and really are worth the extra trouble.

Working out scallops

To make a paper pattern for the scallops,

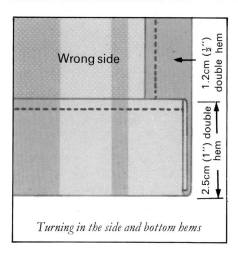
Turning in the side and bottom hems

cut a piece of paper as wide as the curtain fabric and about 30.5cm (12in) deep. A piece of wallpaper or lining paper is ideal for this.

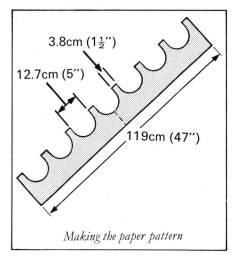
Making the paper pattern

Draw a line across the paper about 7.6cm (3in) down from the upper edge. Decide at this point how deep you want the scallops to be. Draw another line the depth of the scallop below the first line. Now mark the paper vertically down the middle because it is easier to plan scallops on a narrower width. Plan one half of the width first and then trace off another half for accurate placing.

Use a compass and a pencil for drawing scallops and remember that the shape of the scallop will depend on where you place the compass point. Experiment by moving the point until you have a segment that fits your plan. Start drawing the scallops and leave 3.8cm (1½in) between each scallop and approximately 3.8cm (1½in) at each end of the curtain. When all the scallops have been drawn in, cut the scallops out for a pattern.

Making up the curtain

With right side of fabric up, fold over top of the curtain to the depth of the scallops plus 7.6cm (3in) Tack (baste).

Place and pin the prepared paper pattern to the fold and mark around the scallops with tailors' chalk. Remove the pattern and machine stitch on the marked line. Cut out scallops 6mm (¼in) outside the stitching line. Clip into curves and trim corners diagonally.

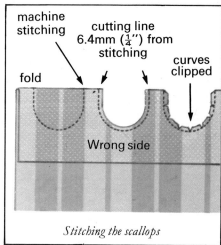
Stitching the scallops

Turn facing to wrong side and press well. Finish the lower edge of the facing with a 1.3cm (½in) hem and slip stitch hem at the sides of the curtain.

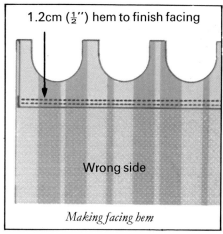
Making facing hem

Sew brass or plastic rings to the top of the scallops using buttonhole twist.

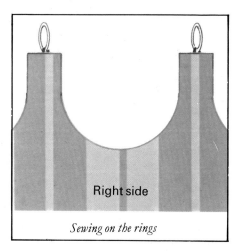
Sewing on the rings

Lined curtains

Lining improves the appearance of all curtains, making them seem fuller and better draped. For curtains hung at windows it also protects them from fading and soiling on the window side and it intensifies their colour against daylight, makes them more opaque and helps keep out draughts (drafts). For curtains used as room dividers, as in the photograph, a matching or contrasting lining makes the curtains equally attractive on both sides.

There are three methods of making lined curtains, depending on where they are

Below *A very useful way of using lined curtains is to create a room-divider. Here, a pair of lined curtains is hung from a pole (rod) with decorative curtain rings. The tie backs are cut from the same fabric, and drape the curtains evenly.*

being used, the type of fabric and the size of the curtains. The quickest method is the machine one but this should only be used for short window curtains in a single width light weight fabric such as cotton and linen-type rayons. For fuller or heavier floor length window curtains (particularly velvet) the hand-stitched method should be used, and for room dividers the reversible method should be followed.

The lining fabric

For curtains to be hung at windows, use a conventional lining fabric, such as sateen. This is sold in white, beige and a few colours in the normal furnishing width of 122cm (48in). Buy the same amount of lining as curtain fabric and wash it before cutting out to allow for shrinkage.

When the curtains are to be used as room dividers, they should be made with equally attractive fabric on each side. This can be the same fabric; in which case you should buy double the amount; or contrasting fabrics of similar weight and type, in which case you should buy the same amount of each fabric. You should also buy double the amount of gathering tape and hooks.

Machine method

1 Cut out the curtain fabric to the right size. Work a line of tacking (basting) down the centre of each length.
2 Cut out the lining fabric, making it 5.1cm (2in) shorter and 7.6cm (3in) narrower for each curtain. Work a line of tacking (basting) down the centre of each length.
3 Make a double hem of 7.6cm (3in)

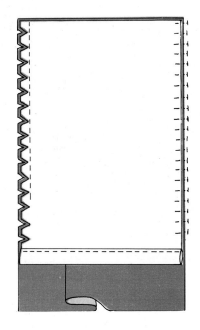

along the bottom of the lining and machine stitch.
4 Lay out the curtain fabric right side up and make a tuck of 7.6cm (3in) down the middle to make it the same width as the lining.
5 Place the lining on the curtain with right sides together so that the top and sides are level. Pin the sides together taking turnings slightly larger than the selvedges on the curtain fabric.
6 Machine stitch to within 5.1cm (2in) of the foot of the lining.
7 Turn the curtain right side out and match the centre point to the centre of the lining. Lay the curtain out flat with the lining side up and centre the lining on the curtain so there is an equal border of curtain showing along both sides. Press.

8 Turn down the top edge of the curtain for 3.8cm (1½in) and tack (baste) through all thicknesses. Attach gathering tape in the same way as for unlined curtains.
9 Hang the curtains for a few days to allow for the fabric dropping, then mark the hemline.

Making a mitred hem

1 Turn up the lower edge of the curtain along the marked hemline. Press lightly.
2 Measure the depth of the hem and turn under half the turning to make a double hem. Press lightly. Mark the position of the second fold on the edge of the curtain (i.e. the stitching line).
3 Unfold the hem completely and fold over the corners diagonally in a line which passes from the stitching line at the side of the curtain, through the junction of the side fold line and the second fold line of the hem, to the edge of the hem. Press.
4 Fold down the side turning of the curtain and catch in position. Turn up the hem along the same folds and pin in position. Tack (baste) and slip stitch. Catch the remaining lining in position. Press

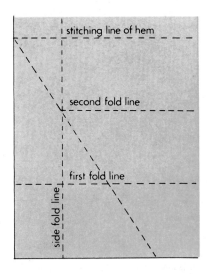

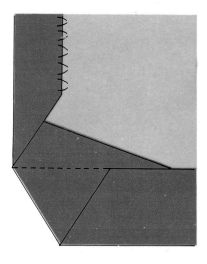

the finished hem and re-hang the curtain.

Hand-stitched method

1 Cut out the curtain fabric and join the widths if necessary. Cut out the lining, making it 5.1cm (2in) shorter than the curtain fabric. Mark the centre point of the top edges if the curtains are a single width. Join the widths, adjusting the turnings to match those on the curtain fabric, and press the curtains open.
2 Make 5.1cm (2in) single turnings on the wrong side along each side edge of the curtains and slip stitch loosely.
3 Make a double hem of 7.6cm (3in) along the bottom of lining and stitch.
4 Lay out the curtain, wrong side up, completely flat on a large smooth surface (the floor is ideal if you haven't a table large enough). Lay the lining, wrong side down, on top of the curtain, matching the centre points of the turnings and so that the top edges are level.
5 If the curtains have more than one fabric width, fold the lining back on to itself down a seam line. Tack (baste) the turning on one side of the seam to the correspond-

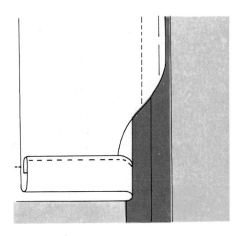

ing turning on the curtain to within 30.5cm (12in) of the bottom. Then lock in the lining as for a single width curtain.

6 If the curtains are made from a single fabric width, fold the lining back down the centre so that the side edges are level. Keeping the lining completely flat, lock it to the curtain (this process prevents the lining from billowing away from the curtain, thus helping it drape and also preventing the lining from dropping).

Locking in the lining

1 Using thread to match the curtain fabric, start 30.5cm (12in) from the bottom of the curtain and work upward. Secure the thread to the fold of the lining and pick up two threads of the curtain fabric. Work along the fold in a blanket stitch, placing the stitches about 5.1cm (2in) apart and keeping the loops loose to avoid puckering. Pick up no more than two threads of curtain fabric so that the stitches will not show on the right side.

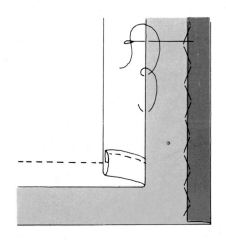

2 When the first line of locking is complete, fold the lining down again and smooth it flat. Then fold it back on itself 45.7cm (18in) away from the first fold and repeat the process. Work across

the width of the curtain in this way, locking the lining to the curtain fabric along the seam lines and about three times to each fabric width.

3 When all the locking is complete, keep the lining and curtain flat and turn the side edges of the lining under to come 3.8cm (1½in) from the edge of the curtain (this measurement can be adjusted if necessary so that the lining completely covers the selvedge of the curtain fabric).

4 Pin in place, placing the pins at right-angles to the edge of the curtains.

5 Slip stitch the fold of the lining loosely to the turning of the curtain by inserting the needle into the fold of the lining and withdrawing it 1.3cm (½in) further on and inserting it immediately into the turning of the curtain and making a stitch on the inside of about 1.3cm (½in). Finish the stitching about 7.6cm (3in) above the hem of the lining.

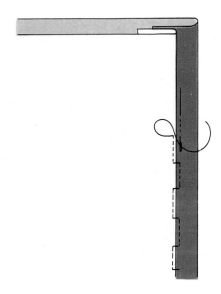

6 Turn up the hem of the curtain, mitering the corners as for the machine method. Slip stitch the remaining part of the lining in position and hang the finished curtains.

Reversible method

The curtains for room dividers are really made like very wide unlined curtains which are then folded in half and joined down the side.

1 Cut and join the fabric for the curtains and the lining, making them the same length.

2 With right sides together, join the lining to the curtain down one of the side edges, taking turnings 1.3cm (½in) wide or the width of the selvedges if this is more.

3 Turn over the top edge of the curtain

and lining and attach curtain tape along the entire width (including the lining).

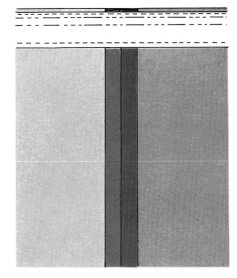

4 Pull up the tape to make the curtain and lining double the required width, plus 2.5cm (1in). The seam joining the lining should be exactly in the centre.

5 With the right side inside, join the lining to the curtain down the remaining side edge. Turn right side out and position the seams exactly at the edges.

6 Insert the curtain hooks along the entire width of the curtain and lining and place them into the hooks of the track alternately from the lining and then the curtain and then the lining and so on. Allow to hang for a couple of days.

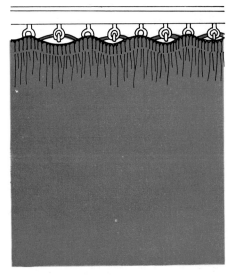

7 Turn up the hem, keeping the bottom of the lining exactly level with the bottom of the curtain. Make double turnings and slip stitch into position.

Styles for tie backs

Simple tie backs can be made from straight strips, cut from the same fabric as the curtains. As a variation, if the curtains are of a patterned fabric, the tie backs can be in a plain fabric which matches one of the colours. Or, if the curtains are in a plain fabric, the tie backs can be made of a patterned fabric to match something else in the room. Straight tie backs can also be made from furnishing braid which is simpler still, as they do not need to be lined or interfaced. For a more draped effect, the tie backs can be cut in a similar way to a curved waist band so that they 'sit' well round the curtain, or they can be made with bound, scalloped or shaped edges for a more decorative finish.

The tie backs are hung with curtain rings of 1.3cm ($\frac{1}{2}$in) diameter, which are sewn to the centre of the short ends of the strips. The rings are placed on to small hooks screwed into the window frame at the required height.

Measuring the tie backs

The most attractive width is between 5.1cm–7.6cm (2in–3in), although you can make them up to 2.5cm (1in) wider if you prefer. To calculate the length, loop a tape measure around the curtains and adjust the length until you have the best effect. This will also give the best position for the tie backs.

Making straight tie backs

1 Cut out two pieces of fabric twice the width of the tie backs plus 2.5cm (1in) for turnings, by the length of the tie backs plus 2.5cm (1in).
2 Cut out two pieces of iron-on interfacing to the exact size of the tie backs.

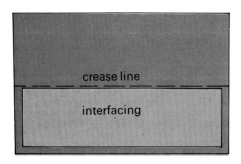

3 Fold the fabric for the tie backs in half lengthwise with the right side out and press firmly along the fold. Open out the pieces and place on the interfacing strips so that one long edge lies along the crease line of the fabric and there is 1.3cm ($\frac{1}{2}$in) margin on the remaining

three sides. Pin in position and iron so that the interfacing adheres to the fabric.
4 Fold the tie backs in half lengthwise again, but this time have the right side inside. Tack (baste) and machine stitch round the three raw edges, taking 1.3cm ($\frac{1}{2}$in) turnings and leaving a small opening in the stitching on the long side.
5 Trim the turnings diagonally across the corners and turn the tie backs right side out.

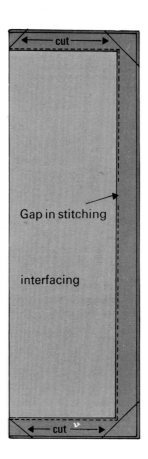

6 Fold under the turnings of the opening, pin and slip stitch the folds together. Tack (baste) round the edges carefully so that the seam is exactly on the edge. Press.
7 Mark the centre of the short edges of the tie backs and sew on the curtain rings with several loose stitches.

8 Screw the hooks into position at the sides of the window and hang tie backs in place.

Braid tie backs

1 Cut the braid to the required length of the tie backs, plus 2.5cm (1in) for turnings.
2 Fold under the turnings at each end and make narrow hems. Slip-stitch the hems.
3 Sew the curtain rings to the centre of the short ends with several loose stitches.

Shaped tie backs

1 Start by making a paper pattern of the shape you require. The simplest way of doing this is to cut a piece of paper about 7.6cm (3in) wider than the required width and about 2.5cm (1in) longer. To make sure the shape is symmetrical, fold the paper in half widthwise to make the strip half the length of the tie back.
2 Draw on the shape for half the tie back from the fold of the paper. Cut around the shape, open it out and try the pattern in position. Adjust the shape if necessary.

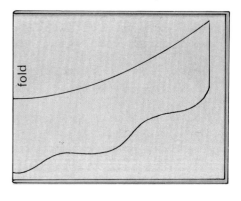

3 Cut out four pieces from the paper pattern, allowing 1.3cm ($\frac{1}{2}$in) all around for turnings. (If you are short of fabric, two pieces may be cut from lining fabric). Cut out two pieces of iron-on interfacing to the exact size of the pattern.
4 Place the interfacing on the wrong side of two of the tie back pieces (or the linings) so there is exactly 1.3cm ($\frac{1}{2}$in) margin all around. Iron firmly so that the interfacing adheres to the fabric.
5 Pin the interfaced pieces to the unstiffened pieces so that the right sides are facing. Tack (baste) and machine stitch taking 1.3cm ($\frac{1}{2}$in) turnings and leaving an opening in the stitching along one edge.
6 Trim the turnings diagonally across the corners and turn the tie backs right side out.
7 Finish off as for straight tie backs.

Above *Roller blinds are bright,*
useful, and easy to make up.
Increasingly popular, they are
ideal in a modern setting, and
are available in many patterns.

Roller blinds

Roller blinds are one of the easiest ways to give a new look to your home. Make your own and you can match them to any room. Roller blinds can easily be made to fit almost any window, using your own fabric and a roller available in kit form.

Measuring for blinds

A roller blind can be hung either inside or outside the window recess, depending on the shape of the window and the frame. If it is to hang inside the recess, check that the window fittings do not protrude far enough to touch the fabric. If the recess is shallow, or the window narrow, hang the blind outside the recess.

Measure the size of the area to be covered by the blind with a wooden yard stick or steel rule, rather than a fabric tape measure, so that the measurements are absolutely accurate.

Measuring inside the recess

1 First measure the width of the recess. The roller should be cut 2.5cm (1in) smaller than this, to allow for the pins and brackets to be fitted at either end. The width of the fabric should be the same as the roller before the pins are attached, plus 5.1cm (2in) for side hems if necessary. Alternatively, the sides can be bound with bias binding, in which case the fabric is cut to the size of the roller.

2 For the length of the blind, measure the height of the recess from the top to the window sill and add 30.5cm (12in) to allow for the fabric to be attached to the roller at the top and for the lath casing at the bottom. This amount ensures that, when the blind is down, there will still be some fabric covering the roller.

Measuring outside the recess

1 Measure the width of the recess and add 15.2cm (6in) to this so that the roller covers the recess well by 7.6cm (3in) on each side. Cut the roller to this length. The width of the fabric should be the same as the roller, plus 5.1cm (2in) for the side hems. No hem allowance is necessary if sides are bound with bias binding.

2 For the length of the blind, measure the height of the blind and add 45.7cm (18in). This allows for the fabric being attached to the roller at the top, for the casing at the bottom, and for the finished blind to be hung about 7.6cm (3in) above the reveal and come down the same amount below it.

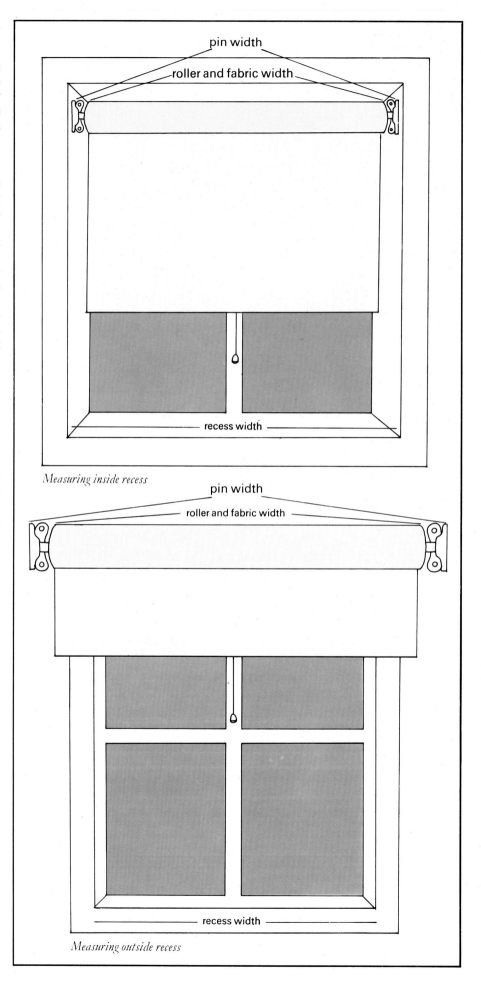

Measuring inside recess

Measuring outside recess

Cutting the fabric

1 It is essential that the fabric is cut accurately on the grain, so that the blind hangs and rolls up smoothly without puckering. The safest way of doing this is to tear the fabric to the required size. Alternatively, withdraw a thread at the right point and then cut along this line.

2 If you have to join more than one width of fabric to get the right size, cut two widths of the same length and then cut one of these in half lengthwise.

If the pattern continues into the selvedge, join each half length along the selvedges to the sides of the main piece by overlapping the edges for 1.3cm ($\frac{1}{2}$in), and machine stitching twice, one down each edge. If the selvedges do not match the fabric trim them off and then join the pieces with machine fell seams.

The fabric

Fabric for roller blinds should be firm and closely woven. Holland (a stiff linen) is widely used and it is available in a variety of widths and colours. Its advantage is that it can be trimmed to the right width and it does not fray, so you do not have to make side hems.

Closely woven cotton, hessian (burlap) and canvas can also be used, although you will need to make side hems, and PVC fabrics in strong, bright colours and patterns are ideal for kitchens and bathrooms.

Making the blind

1 Finish the side edges with bias binding or make hems.

To make the side hems, fold over 2.5cm (1in) on to the wrong side along both edges and press and tack (baste) down unless the fabric is PVC coated. For PVC, crease the fold by hand, and hold in place with adhesive tape rather than using pins.

2 Machine stitch, using a large zig-zag stitch, and positioning the raw edge in the centre of the zig zag.

3 To make the lath casing along the bottom edge, turn under 1.3cm ($\frac{1}{2}$in) on the wrong side. Turn under another

Wrong side of fabric

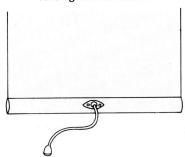

3.8cm ($1\frac{1}{2}$in) and machine stitch.

4 Cut the lath to 1.3cm ($\frac{1}{2}$in) less than the fabric width and insert it into the hem. Stitch up the openings at each side.

5 Thread the cord through the knot holder, and screw this into the centre of the lath on the back of the blind so that the cord hangs down.

Finishing the blind

1 Before you attach the fabric to the roller, it can be sprayed with spray starch to give extra body. Iron flat.

2 Assemble the roller and pins, and screw the brackets in place, following the manufacturer's instructions. If the blind is being attached inside the recess, allow enough room above the brackets to give clearance for the fabric when it is rolled up.

3 The fabric should be attached to the roller so that it hangs next to the window, with the roll towards the room.

Place the prepared fabric right side up on

right

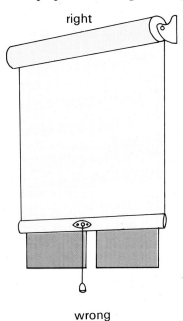

wrong

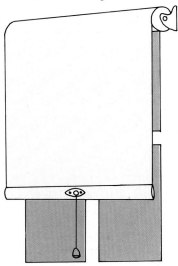

the floor. Lay the roller across the top with the spring mechanism on the left.

4 Attach the fabric to the roller, using a staple gun or row of small tacks, working from the centre toward the edges.

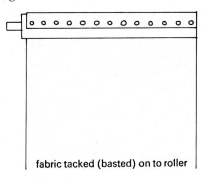

fabric tacked (basted) on to roller

5 Roll up the blind by hand and place it in the brackets. Pull it down and make sure it hangs properly.

6 If it does not roll up smoothly, tension the spring by taking down the blind and re-rolling by hand. Take care not to over-tension it, however, because if it snaps up too quickly, the mechanism may be damaged.

7 Thread the loose end of the cord into the acorn, and the blind is complete.

Cushions

Cushions can be decorative as well as useful. You can easily make an eye-catcher from a simple basic shape with clever use of fabric or trimmings.

Estimating cushions

Plain cushion cover

For a good fit, cover should be slightly smaller all around than cushion pad. For a 45.7cm (18in) square cushion with piped edges you would need 107.9cm (1⅛yds) of 91.4cm (36in) fabric or 57.1cm (⅝yd) of 121.9cm (48in) fabric. The cutting diagrams include fabric for bias, strips for piping and 1.3cm (½in) seams, so allow correspondingly less for an unpiped cover. Measure perimeter of cushion to find amount of piping cord (pre-shrunk).

Boxed cushion covers

First make pattern for top and bottom. Lay cushion flat on a sheet of brown paper and draw around it accurately. For the gusset measure depth of cushion to find depth, then measure all around cushion to find length required. If using piping, double this length to find amount of pre-shrunk piping needed. Add 1.3cm (½in) seam allowance all around cushion and gusset sections. Plan any joins in gusset strip at corners of cushion. If you wish to insert a zipper at the back of cushion, cut back gusset section 2.5cm (1in) deeper.

Bolster cushion

The body piece is made from a rectangle of fabric with two circular ends which can be piped if you wish. For dimensions of rectangle, measure length of bolster, then measure circumference of round end to give you width needed. Cut two circles, each the diameter of bolster for ends, with 1.3cm (½in) seam allowance all around. Also cut out the rectangle with 1.3cm (½in) seam allowance.
For a bolster 66.0cm by 20.3cm (26in by 8in) you will need 91.4cm (1yd) of 91.4cm (36in) wide fabric, 137.1cm (1½yds) pre-shrunk piping cord, 45.7cm (18in) zipper.

Squash cushion cover

Measure the cushion pad and estimate fabric requirements in same way as the box cushion. About 68.6cm (¾yd) is sufficient for an average kitchen chair, without piping.

Piping

Piping cord can be bought in six thicknesses, depending on the purpose for which it is intended. Numbers 1 and 2 are fine cords used mainly for eiderdowns and cushions made of finer fabrics such as silk. Bias strips to cover these should be 3.2cm (1¼in) wide; numbers 3 and 4 are for loose covers and cushions, bias strips for these should be 3.8cm (1½in) wide; numbers 5 and 6 are used for thicker materials where a bolder edge is required, bias strips for these should be 4.4cm (1¾in) wide. Measure length of piping required, then cut bias strips of the appropriate width to the length required, joining as shown in fig. 1. As piping cord can shrink it is advisable to boil cord before using. Cover piping cord with bias strip (fig. 2) using zipper foot on your sewing machine or just tack (baste) if you prefer. 22.9cm (¼yd) of 121.9cm (48in) wide fabric will make about 6.4m (7yds) of 3.8cm (1½in) wide bias strip. Here is a very quick method of joining lengths of bias strips and will give about 4.8m (5¼yds) of 3.8cm (1½in) bias strips from 22.9cm (¼yd) 91.4cm (36in) size fabric (fig. 3). To apply piping, tack (baste) the covered cord to right side of fabric, with stitching lines of piping matching stitching lines of fabric section. Clip outside edges of bias strip at corners and curves (fig. 4). With right sides together stitch other section which is being joined using the zipper foot on your machine.

1. Joining piping cord

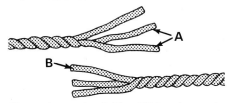

Cut cord to overlap 2.54cm (1in) and unravel and cut away two strands A. Cut away strand B.

Twist remaining ends and stitch together.

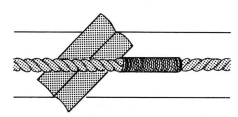

Final join in crosswise strip and cord

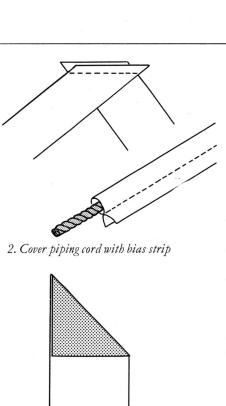

2. Cover piping cord with bias strip

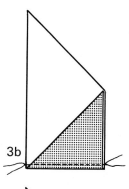

6.4mm (¼″) seam allowance

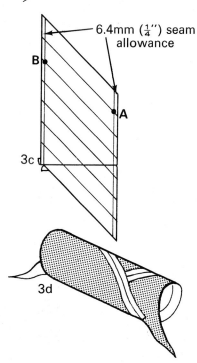

3. Joining lengths of bias strips.
Take a strip of fabric – length of the strip should be at least twice the width.
Fold over the top right hand corner as shown to obtain the crosswise grain. Press (figure 3a)
Cut off this corner and join to lower edge with right sides facing.
After stitching the pieces together press seam open. (figure 3b)
Trim off any selvedges.
Make a ruler in cardboard to the required width of the strips, to be used as a guide. Using a ruler mark the crosswise lines on the right side of the fabric in tailor's chalk, parallel to the top edge. Also mark seam allowances down each side. Mark points A and B carefully as shown. (figure 3c)
Take a pin through the wrong side of fabric at point A and through to point B and pin very accurately with right sides together. Continue pinning along seam. (figure 3d).
Tack (baste), checking that the lines are matching up exactly. Stitch, then press seam open using a sleeve board.
Turn to the right side and start cutting round the spiral at the projecting strip at the top. (figure 3e)
If plenty of fabric is available and no economy necessary, the top right hand corner and the bottom left hand corner can be cut off and thrown aside. This way you will have fewer joins in the strips.

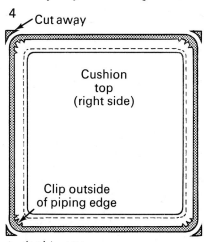

4. Applying piping

Piped Bolster Cushions

When choosing fabric for a bolster cover, avoid large patterns which might prove difficult to match at seams. Cut out body section and two round ends to required size, plus bias strips for piping. With right sides together, stitch long sides of rectangle at each end, leaving space in centre for zipper. Tack (baste) this opening together and press seam. Tack (baste) zipper in position, turn fabric tube right side out and back stitch zipper firmly in place. Turn cover to wrong side again. Prepare piping and stitch to right side of bolster ends. Snip seam allowances of tube and piping end at intervals and stitch circles to tube, right sides together. Turn to right side through zipper opening. If making your own pad, use down-proof cambric for feather and down fillings, otherwise. Make as bolster cover, omitting piping and zipper. Fill through opening in side, then slipstitch opening to close.

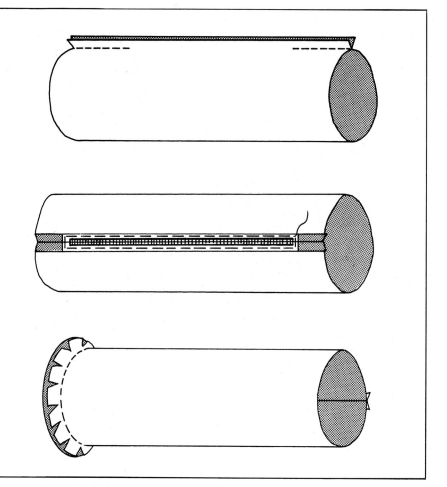

Boxed cushions

Cut out top and bottom cover sections, gusset and bias strips if required for piping. Cut back gusset strip 2.5cm (1in) deeper in inserting zipper. Pin all pieces together around cushion to check fit. Prepare piping.

Cut back gusset in half along the length if using zipper. Stitch seams at each end, leaving space for zipper in centre. Insert zipper. Otherwise, cushion can be fastened with press studs (snaps) or cover can simply be slipped on cushion through a gap left in gusset seam which is then slip stitched together (see diagram). Stitch piping to top and bottom cushion sections snipping piping seam allowance at corners. Stitch gusset seams then stitch gusset section to the piped top section with right sides together. Snip gusset turning at corners. Attach bottom of cushion cover similarly.

Covering foam cushion shapes

These can be bought ready-made in various shapes and sizes. Before making top cover, make an inner cover from strong cambric or sheeting (muslin), using same method.

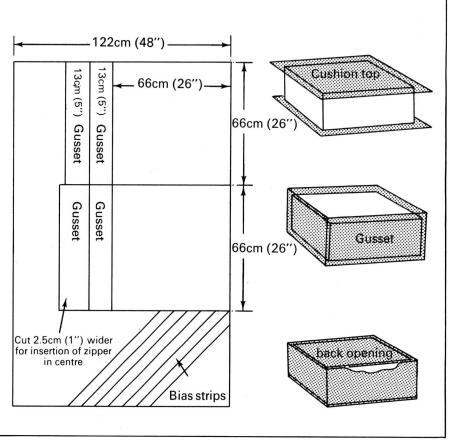

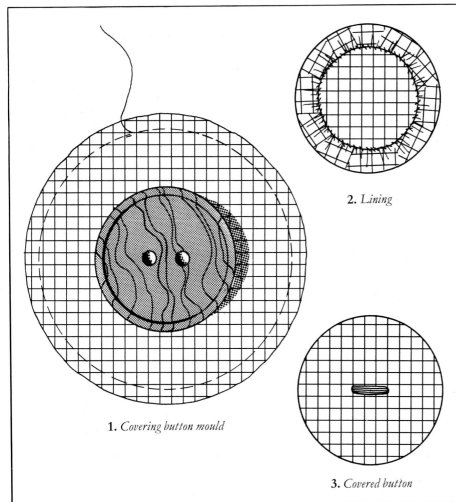

1. *Covering button mould*

2. *Lining*

3. *Covered button*

Buttoned cushions

To make covered buttons, cut circle of fabric 6mm ($\frac{1}{4}$in) larger than button mould. Sew a running stitch around edge of fabric and place mould in centre. Gather until fabric is pulled taut and fasten securely at back. Cover back of button with another smaller circle of fabric with edges turned in and slip stitched in place.

To attach buttons, mark exact positions on top of cushions with crossed pins or tacking (basting) thread. Mark corresponding positions on underside where small buttons with two eyes are stitched to anchor the larger ones. Fit cover on cushion. To sew on the buttons, use four thicknesses of a strong buttonhole twist and a long darning needle. Sew through eye of small button, through cushion from back of button position, through back of covered button, back through cushion and other eye of small button. Knot threads at back, drawing threads tightly so that the top button sinks into cushion. Knot firmly.

Below *Several styles of cushions are shown, in both modern and more traditional settings. You can make them a really striking feature of a room.*

37

Simple cushion making

Add an individual character to any room with cushions sewn by you in your own choice of fabric. Make them in a variety of shapes, sizes and textures, in colours to blend with your decor. Cushions also make a useful way to display other techniques, such as patchwork.

The fabric

Most fabrics can be used for flat cushion covers (those without welts), although very fine fabrics usually need backing and can be difficult to work on. If you intend to pipe the edges of a cushion do not use a loosely woven fabric as the cord will show through. How much fabric? For a plain (unpiped) flat cushion decide on the size of your cushion cover and allow at least twice this amount, plus 1.3cm ($\frac{1}{2}$in) extra all around for turnings. For a 30.5cm (12in) flat square or round finished cover you will need a piece of fabric at least 33cm x 66cm (13in x 26in). Allow an extra 45.7cm ($\frac{1}{2}$yd) of fabric if you intend to pipe the edge of the cover. This amount of fabric, although some

wastage is involved, avoids too many joins in the casing strip.

For a well-filled, professional looking cushion make the cover 1.3cm (½in) smaller all around than its pad.

Plain flat square cushion
You will need
A cushion pad.

Fabric as above.
Matching thread.
Keeping the grain straight, cut two pieces of fabric to the calculated size.

With right sides together, tack (baste) and machine stitch around three sides.

On the fourth side fold down the seam allowances on to the wrong side of each section and press. Trim the stitched

corners (fig. 1). Make the turnings neat and turn right side out. Press.

Insert the pad and slip stitch the opening neatly by hand. These stitches can be easily removed when the cover is washed. Rectangular cushions are made in the same way.

Plain flat round cushion
It is necessary to make a paper pattern to make sure of an accurate curve. Draw a semi circle on a large sheet of paper. To do this, attach a piece of string to a pin, and a pencil to the other end. Pierce paper firmly with pin, and draw your circle, adjusting the radius to different sizes of circles. Make the distance between pin and pencil equal to the radius of the finished cover, plus 1.3cm (½in).

1. *Square cushion stitched on three sides with corners trimmed*

You will need:
A cushion pad.
Fabric as above.
Matching thread.
Fold fabric in half lengthwise along the grain. Place the pattern with the straight edge to the fold. Pin into place and cut along the curved line only. Mark grain line along fold with tacking (basting). Cut another piece of fabric in the same way.

With right sides together, grain lines matching, place the two sections together. Tack (baste) and machine stitch 1.3cm (½in) from the edge all round the cover, leaving an opening of about one quarter of the circumference.

Clip small V-shapes to within 3mm (⅛in) from the stitching at 2.5cm (1in) intervals all around (fig. 2).

Finish off as for a square cover.

Left *A colourful pile of cushions, all simple to make, and using fabrics with skill and imagination. As well as plain colours and basic shapes, you can experiment with different kinds of patchwork, or select really unusual fabric patterns.*

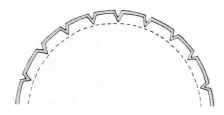

2. *Round cushion stitched and clipped*

Piped cushions

Piping should be attached before the cushion cover is made up. It is not a good idea to pipe flat round cushion covers as these do not keep a good shape when the pad is inserted.

Zipper foot To attach piping successfully by machine it is necessary to use a zipper foot on your sewing machine. This is made in one piece, instead of split as with the standard foot, enabling the stitching to be worked close to the piping.

The cushion cover is usually inserted into the machine with its bulk on the left and the turnings of the seam under the foot. The needle should be to the left of the foot which is pressed up hard against the

piping cord. Keep the foot in this position throughout the sewing. At the corners, leave the needle down, lift the foot and turn the fabric around to the new position. Lower foot and continue sewing.

Piping consists of a cord covered with bias-cut strips of fabric and is stitched into a seam.

Piping cord is usually cotton and made up of three strands. It comes in a range of thicknesses and number 2 or 3 is most suitable for cushion covers. As the cord is liable to shrink, buy about 23cm (¼yd) extra. Boil the cord for about 5 minutes and dry it thoroughly before use to ensure that it is fully shrunk.

Cut and join enough 3.8cm (1½in) wide bias strips to fit the perimeter of the cover, plus 10.1cm (4in).

Lay piping cord, slightly longer than the strip, centrally along the wrong side of this strip. Fold the edges together, with the cord in the middle. Tack (baste) or machine stitch casing firmly around cord to within 2.5cm (1in) of each end, keeping the stitching as close as possible

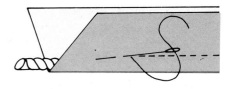

3. *Casing tacked (basted) around cord*

to the piping (fig. 3).

Starting in the middle of a side, pin the casing all round the edge on the right side of one cover piece. The raw edges of the folded casing must be level with the raw edges of the cover. At each corner, clip into the casing seam allowance to within 3mm (⅛in) of the tacking (basting) stitches of the casing. This will make the piping lie flat (fig. 4).

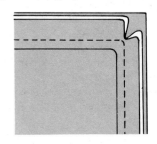

4. *Casing pinned in place*

To make a neat join in the piping unfold the untacked (unbasted) portion of the casing at each end and overlap them by 1.3cm (½in). Adjust the overlap to fit the cushion cover exactly. Join the ends as for bias strips, trimming to 6mm (¼in).

Overlap the cord for 2.5cm (1in) and trim off the excess. Unravel 2.5cm (1in) at each end and cut away two strands from one end and one strand from the other. Overlap and twist together the remaining three ends and stitch or bind them firmly

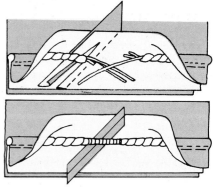

5. *Making a join in casing and cord*

(fig. 5). Fold over casing and tack (baste) around joined cord. Tack (baste) piping to cushion. Place the second cover piece on top of the piped piece, with right sides together and enclosing the piping. Tack (baste) and stitch the cover together along three sides.

Two ways to insert a zipper

When a cover needs to be removed frequently for washing you may prefer to insert a permanent type of fastening such as a zipper.

Zippers are best kept for use on cushions with straight sides as a zipper faster is inclined to distort the shape of a round cushion.

The methods given here are for piped cushions but plain cushions can be treated in the same way.

Zipper stitched by hand This is a very neat way of putting in a zipper.

Make up the cushion in the usual way but stitch along the fourth side for 2.5cm (1in) at each end. Fasten off the stitching securely. Turn the cover right side out. Press under the turning along the piped edge if piping has been used.

Place the piped edge over the right side of the closed zipper so that the folded edge of the turning lies centrally along the teeth of the zipper.

On the right side of the cover tack (baste) along the space between the piping and cover (fig. 6).

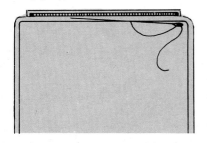

6. Tacking (basting) along the gulley

Fold under the unpiped edge of the opening and put it on to the zipper so that it meets the piped edge. Tack (baste) in position close to the edge of the zipper teeth, curving the stitching into the fold at the top and bottom.

Using double sewing thread, prick stitch the zipper to the cover along the tacked (basted) line. Prick stitch is like a spaced backstitch, but on the right side of the fabric the stitches should be extremely small (fig. 7).

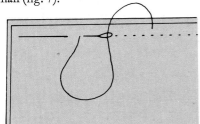

7. Working prick stitch

Zipper stitched by machine. With the cover inside out, place the zipper face downwards on the piped edge of the opening, with the teeth as close as possible to the piping cord.

Tack (baste) and machine stitch the zipper to the turning and piping only, close to the teeth, using a zipper foot (fig. 8).

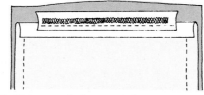

8. Zipper stitched to piped edge

Turn the cover through to the right side and place the other folded edge over the zipper to meet the piped edge.

Tack (baste) and machine stitch the cover to the zipper tape 1cm (⅜in) from the fold: take the stitching across to the fold at each end (fig. 9).

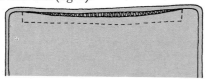

9. Zipper machine stitched in place

Undo the zipper, turn cover to the wrong side and snip into the stitched-down turning at each end.

If you prefer, the zipper can be inserted before the other three sides are stitched.

Cushion pads

Many large stores sell square and oblong cushion pads in a wide range of sizes. It is, however, quite possible to make your own pads in the size and shape you want.

Filling. Down is the most luxurious and most expensive filling and feathers are a good alternative, but many people today prefer to use a synthetic filling which has the advantage of being washable.

Shredded foam and foam chips are cheaper fillings and are washable. However, these can give a lumpy look and foam tends to become hard after a time.

Pad covers. These can be made from sheeting, calico (muslin) or any inexpensive, firmly-woven fabric, but if you choose feathers or down for the filling it is essential to buy a down proof fabric for the pad cover.

Making up. Make the cover in the same way as a plain cushion cover, remembering that it should be 1.3cm (½in) larger all around than the outer cushion cover. Turn through to the right side and press. Stuff the cover with filling so that it is plump but not hard, paying particular attention to the corners. Pin, tack (baste) and stitch close to the edge.

The basic bias

Finding the bias (cross). *Check that the edges of the fabric are level with the straight of grain. Fold fabric diagonally so that the selvedge is level with the cross-wise threads. Press in this fold, without stretching it, and cut along the fold line.*

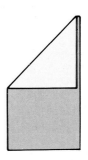

Cutting bias strips. *Cut along the bias fold line, with tailor's chalk or pins, mark off strips of the desired width from this edge. Use a cardboard strip of the correct width to do this accurately. Cut the short ends of each strip so that they slant the same way and are level with the straight of grain.*

Joining bias strips. *To maintain the stretchiness, the seams joining strips must lie on the straight of grain. Place the strips at right angles to each other, with right sides together and short edges level. Tack (baste) and stitch, taking 6mm (¼in) turnings. Press open the seam and trim off the protruding corners.*

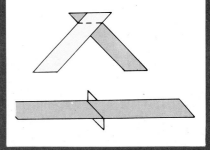

Squab cushions

Fabrics for squab cushions should be firm so that they do not pull or stretch at the seams.

Making squab

You must first make a pattern of the chair seat itself and cut out a cushion pad from a block of foam about 3.8cm (1½in) deep and a little larger than the size of your chair seat (these foam shapes can be bought from furnishing departments).

Lay a sheet of newspaper across chair seat and mark around front and side edges of seat, mark shape around struts at back of chair so seat will fit snugly. Check fit before cutting final paper pattern (fold this in half lengthwise to ensure that sides are uniform).

Mark position of back chair legs on pattern. Lay pattern on foam, draw around with a ballpoint pen and cut out shape with a bread knife. (You can make a flatter cushion without a gusset from a thinner sheet of foam which can be cut with scissors.)

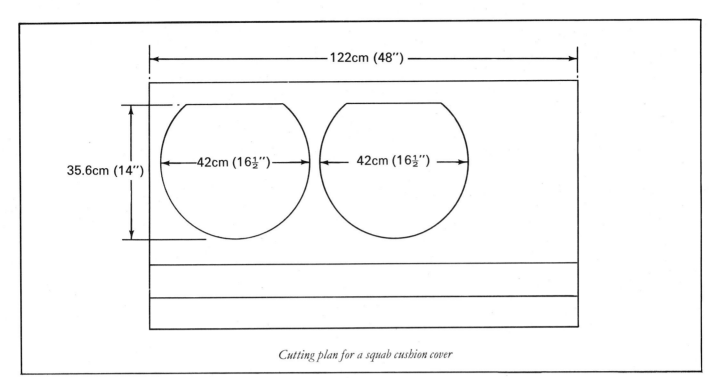

Cutting plan for a squab cushion cover

Placing ties on a squab cushion cover

Making cover

Cut top and bottom seat sections and gusset strip from fabric, allowing 1.3cm ($\frac{1}{2}$in) seams. Pin gusset around edge of cover to check fit. When you are sure it fits exactly, stitch seams and press. For ties, take 91.4cm (1yd) of 1.3cm ($\frac{1}{2}$in) wide straight tape and cut in half. Fold each piece in half and place tapes on right side of bottom cover piece to correspond with chair legs as shown. With right sides together, stitch top cover piece to gusset, clipping seams on curves. Stitch lower cover piece to gusset, taking in tapes and leaving an opening in centre of back seam to insert cushion pad. Turn to right side, insert cushion pad and slip stitch opening to close.

Toggle-fastened squab

Cut cushion and cover in exactly the same way as before, but fasten to chair back with loops and wooden toggles. For loops, cut four strips of fabric, each about 21.6cm ($8\frac{1}{2}$in) by 3.8cm ($1\frac{1}{2}$in) (depending on thickness of fabric and chair strut). Fold in long raw edges 1cm ($\frac{3}{8}$in) and press. Fold again along the length, wrong sides together to form a rouleau. Fold two of the strips double and stitch again leaving loops at ends for toggles. Attach prepared fastenings in pairs to top of cover before stitching gusset in same way as for tape-fastened cushion. Finish cover as before, then sew on wooden toggles and slip through loops.

Round cushions & bolsters

You will need:
A cushion pad.
Fabric for cover.
Piping cord (optional).

To make a cushion. Make a circular paper pattern for the top and bottom of the cushion to the finished size, using the pin and string method.

Pin the pattern to the fabric, following the cutting chart, and cut out a top and bottom piece in fabric, not forgetting to add 1.3cm (½in) seam allowance all around. Cut a strip for the welt to the required depth, by the length of the circumference of the circular pattern, plus 1.3cm (½in) seam allowance all around. (If you have enough fabric it is advisable to allow a little extra on this length which can be trimmed away later if necessary.)

Fold the top and bottom pieces in half and mark the centre back of each piece with thread.

On the welt piece work a line of stitching along each long edge on the seamline. Snip into these edges at 2.5cm (1in) intervals, almost to the stitching. This ensures a good fit when the welt is attached to the top and bottom pieces.

With right sides together, pin one long edge of the welt to the top piece, 1.3cm (½in) from the edge. Start pinning at the centre back, matching the centre back mark with a point 1.3cm (½in) from one short end. Continue pinning until the welt is pinned right around the top and then pin in the welt seam (fig.2).

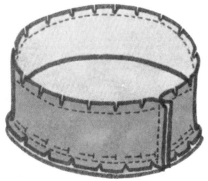

1. *The welt pinned on to a round cushion top with welt seam pinned in*

Stitch the welt seam and trim the seam allowance on the second short end to 1.3cm (½in) if necessary.

Tack (baste) and stitch the welt to the top, taking 1.3cm (½in) turnings.

Snip 'V'-shaped notches almost to the stitching at 2.5cm (1in) intervals in the circular piece and press the turnings onto the welt.

Pin the bottom piece to the welt, making sure that the grain runs the same way as on the top section. Tack (baste) and stitch, taking 1.3cm (½in) seams, leaving about one third of the edge unstitched to turn through. Notch and press turnings as before.

Turn cover to the right side, insert pad and slip stitch opening.

Square cushions
You will need:
A cushion pad.
Fabric for cover.
Piping cord (optional).
Zipper (optional).

To make the cushion. Cut out the pieces for top, bottom and welt of cushion along the grain to the finished size plus seam allowance.

Take two side strips and join them along one short edge taking 1.3cm (½in) turnings. Taper stitching into the corners 1.3cm (½in) from the beginning and end of each seam (fig.3). Join the

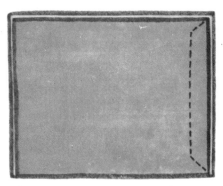

2. *Two welt strips stitched together before attaching welt to a square top*

other strips to these two in the same way to make a continuous strip for the welt. Press turnings to one side.

With right sides together, pin the top section of the cover onto the welt, matching corners of the top to welt seams. Tack (baste) and stitch (fig. 4).

Attach the bottom piece to the welt in the same way, but leave one side open to turn through. Make sure that the grain

3. *The top section of a square cushion cover stitched to the welt.*

runs in the same direction on the top and bottom.

Turn cover to the right side, insert pad and slip stitch opening.

Bolsters
The basic bolster shape is cylindrical, and can be piped or decorated with braid, or other trimming.

The fabric. Choose a closely woven, medium or heavyweight fabric, such as velvet, corduroy, firm tweed, linen or heavy cotton. A loosely woven fabric like soft tweed is unsuitable as it will pull at the seams.

How much fabric? Decide on the length and the diameter of the ends. You will need enough fabric to cut a piece to the length of the finished bolster, plus 2.5cm (1in) for turnings, by the length of the finished circumference of the ends plus at least 2.5cm (1in) for seams, and two circles with a diameter 2.5cm (1in)

larger than that of the finished ends. Draw the pieces to scale on a cutting layout to calculate the amount of fabric required.

Piping. This should be made up and attached to the ends before joining them to the body section.

Zipper. If you wish to use a zipper fastener insert this into the seam of the body section before the ends are stitched into place.

Bolster pads

Soft bolster pads can be bought ready – made in a limited size range. If you wish to make your own pad, make the cover in the same way as the outer cover but do not add piping. It should be 1.3cm ($\frac{1}{2}$in) larger all around than the outer cover.

Firm bolster. Foam rubber pads are sold without covers. It is advisable to make an inner cover for a foam rubber

pad for the reasons described for a cushion with a welt and the same construction techniques apply.

To make a bolster

You will need:
Fabric as above.
Piping (optional).
Zipper (optional).
A bolster pad.

Make a circular paper pattern the size of the finished ends.

Pin the pattern to the fabric, following the cutting layout, and cut out the two ends, not forgetting to add 1.3cm ($\frac{1}{2}$in) seam allowance all around. Cut a strip for the body section of the finished length, plus 2.5cm (1in) for seams, by the length of the circumference of the circular pattern, plus 2.5cm (1in) for the seams. (If you have enough fabric it is advisable to allow a little extra on this measurement which can be trimmed off after joining

if necessary.)

Fold and mark the ends as for the top and bottom of a circular cushion.

On the body section work a line of stitching on the seamlines at the sides of the bolster.

Make 'V'-shaped notches at 2.5cm (1in) intervals almost to this line of stitching. This makes it possible to ease the body section off to the ends.

Stitch the body seam, leaving an opening of half to three quarters of its length in the centre to turn through.

Pin the body section to the ends as if fitting the welt onto the top of a circular cushion (fig. 2).

Tack (baste) and stitch the ends into place taking 1.3cm ($\frac{1}{2}$in) turnings.

Make 'V'-shaped notches at 2.5cm (1in) intervals on the circular pieces and press the turnings onto the body section.

Turn cover to the right side and insert pad. Slip stitch opening.

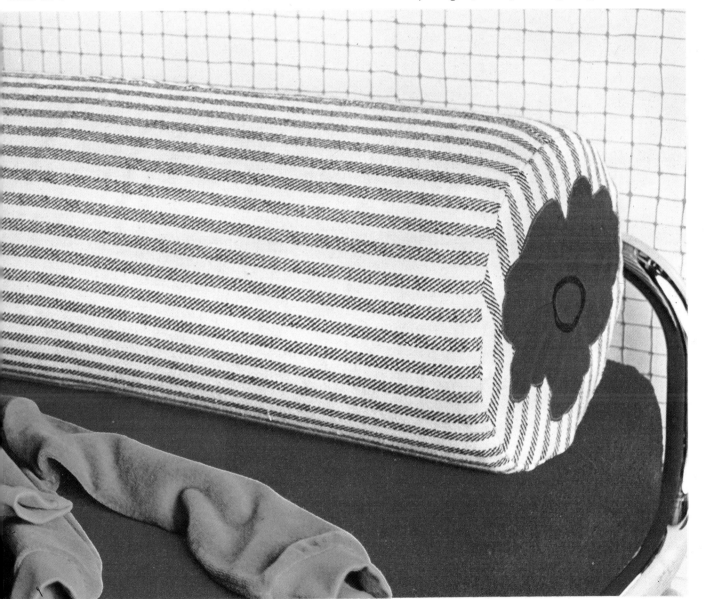

Box cushions

Box cushions are block-shaped cushions with squared-off edges. They are normally made from foam-rubber pads and are often used on the seats and backs of chairs in place of traditional upholstery. They also make good floor cushions.

The pad

If you are buying your own foam pad to make box cushions, check that it is of the correct quality foam for your purpose. To give the best wear, seat cushions should be of a higher density than back cushions and for comfort they should be 7.6cm–10cm (3–4in) thick. Back cushions can be 5.1cm–7.6cm (2–3in) thick.

The fabric

If the cushions are to be used regularly, buy a medium-weight furnishing fabric recommended by the manufacturer for loose covers. It is also advisable to make an inner cover which protects the foam and prevents the main cover from sticking to it. This inner cover can be of calico (muslin), curtain lining or any lightweight cotton. There are two methods of making a cover for a box cushion. Use method one for plain fabrics and method two for patterned or pile fabrics or if you want a piped edge.

Making a cutting chart

The simplest way of estimating the amount of fabric you need is to draw a cutting chart to scale. To do this, draw a straight line to represent the width of your fabric. Draw two more lines at right angles to each end of this. Then draw on the pieces of the cover according to which of the two following methods you are using. Complete the rectangle after the last piece. Measure the length of the rectangle to give the amount of fabric required.

Method 1

1 Measure the width and length of the top of the pad and add on twice the depth plus 2.5cm (1in) each way for turnings. Draw on one piece of this size for the main section of the cover.
2 Draw a second piece equal to the width by the length of the pad, plus 2.5cm (1in) each way for the bottom section of the cover.

Method 2

1 Draw two pieces equal to the width by the length of the pad plus 2.5cm (1in) each way for the top and bottom

sections of the cover.
2 Measure the depth of the pad and draw strips of this width to fit the front and sides of the pad, plus 2.5cm (1in) each way. Draw a fourth strip 2.5cm (1in) wider by the length of the back of the pad, plus 2.5cm (1in). The short edges of all the strips should be parallel with the selvedges so that the pattern will be the right way up on the finished cover.
3 Allow an extra 45.7cm (18in) for the piping casing. For the piping cord, measure the perimeter of the pad and double it allowing an extra 30cm (12in) for shrinkage and joining.
To make the covers easy to remove for cleaning, a zipper can be inserted along the back section in both methods. Buy one which is 1.3cm ($\frac{1}{2}$in) shorter than the width of the pad.

First method
Cutting out

Cut out two pieces of fabric to the sizes given in the cutting chart.

Making up

1 On the larger piece, measure in from the corners in both directions the depth of the pad plus 1.3cm ($\frac{1}{2}$in) and mark.

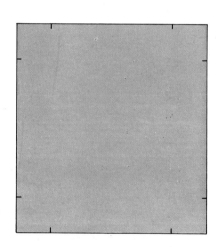

2 Make a dart at each corner by folding the adjacent edges together diagonally so that the marks match and the right sides are inside.

Right *A long box cushion is used here to make a bench seat more comfortable. This is only one of the uses to which box cushions can be put. Try them as floor cushions, and as chair seats or backs as extra firm support.*

46

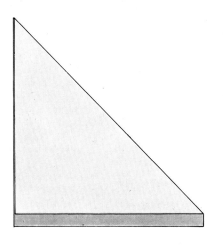

3 Starting 1.3cm (½in) from the raw edges, stitch up from the marks to the fold on the straight grain of the fabric. Trim off the corner to within 6mm (¼in) of the stitching. Press the turnings to one side and overcast them if the fabric is likely to fray.

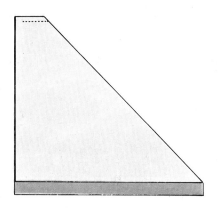

4 With the wrong sides of the fabric facing out, fit the smaller piece to the edges of the larger piece, matching the corners to the darts. Stitch around taking 1.3cm (½in) turnings and leaving an opening for the zipper in the back edge.

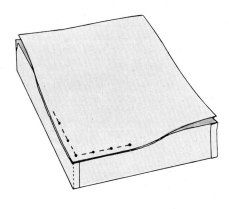

5 Press the seams and turn right side

out. Finish the opening with a zipper.

Second Method
Note cut out and make up pieces so that the design or pile runs from the back to the front on the top and bottom sections of the cover and from top to bottom on the side strips. Any motif should be placed centrally.

Cutting out
Cut out the pieces on the straight grain to the sizes given in the cutting chart.

Making up
1 Join the side strips to each side of the front strip along the short edges, taking 1.3cm (½in) turnings. Taper the stitching into the corners 1.3cm (½in) from the beginning and end of each seam.

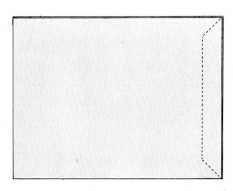

2 Cut the fourth strip in half lengthwise and re-join it for 1.9cm (¾in) at each end, taking 1.3cm (½in) turnings. Insert a zipper into the remaining opening. Attach this strip to the ends of the other strip, taking 1.3cm (½in) turnings and tapering the stitching as before. Press the turnings to one side.

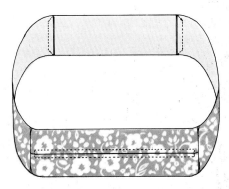

3 If you are having piped edges, cut and make the casing for the cord allowing enough to fit twice around the edge of the strip. Attach it to each edge of the strip taking 1.3cm (½in) turnings. Clip into

the turnings of the casing in line with each seam of the strip.

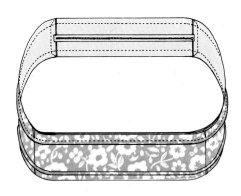

4 With the wrong side of the strip facing out, fit the top edge to the perimeter of the top section, matching the seams of the strip to the corners. Tack (baste) and machine stitch as close to the piping as possible. Overcast the edges of the turnings together if the fabric is likely to fray and press the turnings down on to the strip.

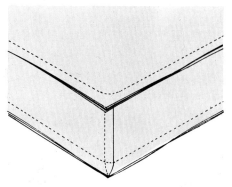

5 Still with the wrong side facing out, turn the strip so that the open side is uppermost. Fit the bottom section of the cover to this edge in the same way as before. Press and turn the finished cover right side out.

Right *Giant, squashy cushions make a cheap and attractive alternative to conventional furniture. Make this huge, segmented cushion in a riot of brilliant colours for a contrasting effect, or in subtle, toning shades for a restful room. These cushions are particularly suitable for children, who love to snuggle comfortably into their depths. If you are planning to make one for the nursery, choose really bright, primary colours in a hard wearing fabric.*

Giant floor cushion

Giant, squashy cushions make a cheap and attractive alternative to conventional furniture. Make this huge, segmented cushion in a riot of contrasting colours for a brilliant effect, or in subtle, toning shades for a restful room.

You will need:
91.4cm, 1.5m (1yd, 60in) wide jersey in navy.
91.4cm, 1.5m (1yd, 60in) wide jersey in beige.
91.4cm, 1.5m (1yd, 60in) wide jersey patterned in beige/brown.
or
1m (1¼ yds) of the same colours in 91.4cm (36in) wide fabric.
cans of Polybeads (pre-expanded polystyrene beads) amounting to 6.7ltr (12pt).

Making the cushion
Draw up a paper pattern from the graph, in which one square equals 2.5cm (1in). Cut one bottom section and one top section from the navy jersey. Cut two navy side segments, two beige side segments and two patterned side segments. With right sides together, pin one long side of a navy segment to one long side of a beige segment. Tack (baste) and machine stitch, taking 1.3cm (½in) seam allowance. Stitch a second 3mm (⅛in) in from the first, for strength. Pin the long side of a patterned segment to the beige segment, and stitch in the same way. Continue alternating the segments until a circular shape is formed.
With right sides together, pin and tack (baste) the top section in position. Stitch the seam twice, as for the sides. Pin in the bottom section and stitch in the same way around five sides. Trim seams and press flat. Turn the cushions through to the right side.

Preparing the filling
To prepare the beads, take a large saucepan with a close-fitting lid. Check how many pints it holds. Leave 5cm (2in) of water in the bottom of the pan, and bring it to the boil. When the water is boiling, pour in one heaped teaspoonful of beads for every pint of the saucepan's capacity. Stir the beads after one minute and again after three minutes, replacing the lid securely each time. After four minutes' 'cooking' the beads are ready. Ladle the beads into the drying bag supplied, and repeat the process.
Close the neck of the drying bag and leave the beads to dry for four days in a well-ventilated place.

Filling the cushion
Use a rubber band to attach one end of the cardboard tube supplied with the beads to the drying bag. Push the other end of the tube through the unstitched cushion seam and pour in the beads. Fill the cushion two-thirds full. Pin the final seam and stitch it. It is worth keeping the cardboard tube and drying bag for removing the beads when the cover needs to be cleaned. The beads must be removed before cleaning of course.

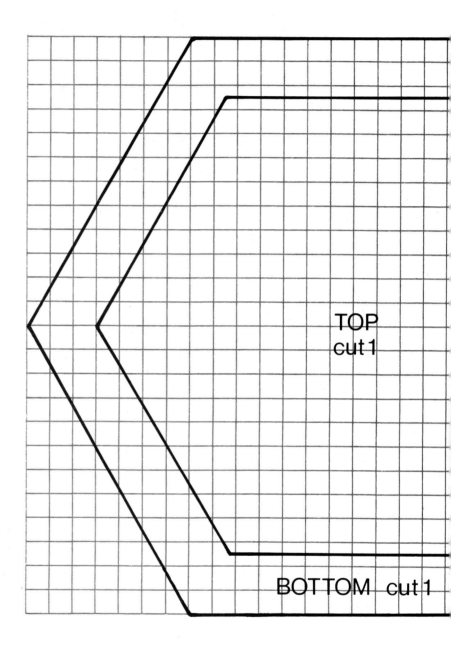

graph pattern for floor cushion

one square = 2·54 cm (1in)

seam allowance included

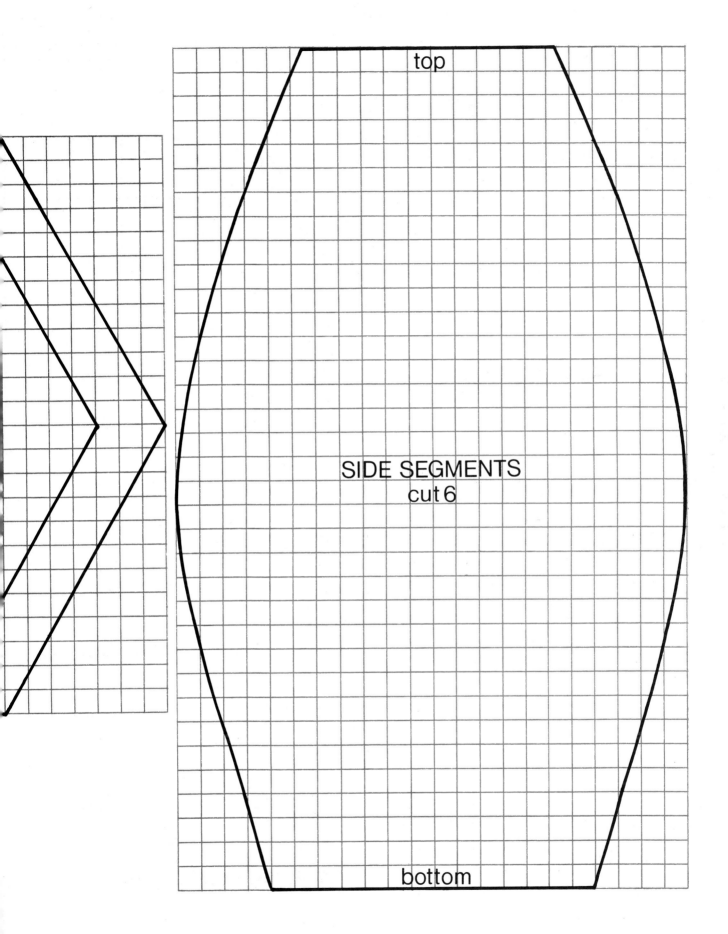

top

SIDE SEGMENTS
cut 6

bottom

Animal cushions

Animal cushions are delightful. The shapes are simple and the children will find them fun.

You will need:

0.45m (½yd) of 91.4cm (36in) fabric (a cotton polyester gaberdine is ideal) in each of the following colours: royal blue, emerald green, bright pink, mauve, yellow.
0.70m (¾yd) of 91.4cm (36in) fabric with red and white stripes.
0.25m (¼yd) of 91.4cm (36in) fabric with red spots on white background.
0.25m (¼yd) of 91.4cm (36in) fabric with white spots on orange background.
0.45m (½yd) of 91.4cm (36in) fabric with green and white stripes.
0.25m (¼yd) of 91.4cm (36in) fabric with pink and white checks.
Scraps of plain red and plain white fabric.
4 packets Vilene Bondaweb (Magic Polyweb).
Graph paper for making the pattern.
Mercerized sewing thread, 1 spool each of bright red, mauve, emerald green, pink.
Stranded embroidery cotton, 1 skein black.
Cushion pads – one in each of the following measurements: 35.5cm (14in) square; 40.5cm (16in) square; 30.5cm x 40.5cm (12in x 16in); 30.5cm x 76cm (12in x 30in); two pads 35.5cm x 46cm (14in x 18in).

Making the pattern

Lay the graph paper flat and place one piece of Vilene Bondaweb (Magic Polyweb) on top with the paper side facing up. Use paper clips to hold the two together so they will not move.
Using the graph paper as a guide only, draw the pattern pieces on to the paper side of the Bondaweb (Polyweb) to scale, 1 square — 1.3cm square (½in square). Cut around the pattern pieces roughly, leaving a margin of about 1.3cm (½in).

The elephant cushion

From the royal blue fabric cut out a rectangle 71cm x 37cm (28in x 14½in).
Set iron to medium-hot temperature and lay the red and white spotted fabric with

Left An appealing collection of cushions decorated with animal motifs will enchant any child. The basic shapes are very simple, and easy to make, while the patterns for the animals are cut out from the graph overleaf.

the wrong side facing up. Press the fabric to remove all creases and place the pattern for the elephant's body onto the fabric, paper side facing up.
Iron firmly using a steam iron or damp cloth and put aside to cool.
Repeat this process with the red fabric and the piece for the elephant's ear. Mark the elephant's mouth and eye on the red fabric.
When quite cool, cut around the pencil lines on Bondaweb (Polyweb). Peel off the paper (a film of bonding adhesive is left on the wrong side of the pieces).
Lay the blue fabric flat on the ironing board with the shorter sides to left and right. Iron to remove all creases and place the piece for the body centrally on the right hand half of the fabric, wrong side down.
Pin into position and iron firmly, using a steam iron or damp cloth.
Place on the piece for the ear, overlapping the body for the amount shown on the pattern. Pin into place and iron firmly.
Lightly mark the position of the eye and mouth and the extension lines of the legs on the body with pencil.
Using the red cotton, sew around the raw edge of the body, and ear and along the pencil line of the legs, using a fine button-hole stitch or a narrow, close machine zig-zag stitch.
Cut roughly around the piece for the eye, leaving a 1.3cm (½in) margin. Place the eye piece into position and stitch by hand along the pencil line, using close buttonhole stitch. Trim off the excess fabric close to the stitching. Do the same with the mouth piece.
Finish the elephant's eyes with three strands of embroidery cotton, using stem stitch.
To finish the cushion cover, fold the fabric in half with short sides together and wrong sides outside. Stitch along the top and bottom taking 1.3cm (½in) turnings, leaving the side edge open. Turn through to right side and press.
Insert the 35.5cm (14in) square cushion pad, pushing it well into the corners. Turn under 1.3cm (½in) on the edges of the opening and slip stitch the folds together.

The giraffes cushion

From the emerald green fabric cut a rectangle 42cm x 81.5cm (16½in x 32in). Mark the centre line in both directions.
Cut out the giraffes after ironing on the Bondaweb (Polyweb) patterns in the same way as for the elephant. Use pencil to draw the pieces for the eyes on the edge of the spare green fabric.

Cut around the giraffes exactly and then iron them to the right hand side of the green fabric.
Sew the giraffes to the green fabric using green thread and a close buttonhole stitch or zig-zag stitch.
Mark the positions for the eyes and mouth lightly in pencil.
Sew on the eyes using two strands of embroidery cotton and a close buttonhole stitch. Embroider the eyelashes and mouth using stem stitch.
Finish the cushion pad as for the elephant, using the 40.5cm (16in) square pad.

The zebra cushion

From the bright pink fabric cut a rectangle 37cm x 91cm (14½in x 36in). Mark the centre lines in both directions. From the green and white striped fabric cut the body for the zebra in the same way as for the elephant. From the spare green fabric cut the tail and head pieces. Apply the body, then the head and tail to the right hand half of the pink fabric, overlapping them for the amount indicated on the shaded area on the pattern.
Using the green thread, sew the pieces to the pink fabric using a close buttonhole or zig zag stitch.
On a scrap of white fabric, draw the shape of the eye. Cut around leaving a 1.3cm (½in) margin. Sew it to the face with a close buttonhole stitch using two strands of black embroidery cotton.
Finish the face by embroidering the eyelashes, pupil, mouth and nostril with stem stitch.
Finish the cover in the same way as for the elephant, using one of the 35.5cm x 46cm (14in x 18in) cushion pads.

The lion cushion

From the mauve fabric cut a rectangle 42cm x 99cm (16½in x 39in). Mark the centre line in both directions.
From the remaining bright pink fabric, cut out the lion's body. From the checked fabric cut the lion's head.
Using a pencil, lightly mark the features of the face on the right side.
Lay out the mauve fabric with the short sides to your left and right and apply the lion's body centrally onto the right hand half.
Add the head, overlapping it for the amount shown on the pattern. Sew the pieces to the ground fabric using mauve cotton. Embroider the features of the face using two strands of black embroidery cotton and stem stitch.
Finish the cushion, using one of the 35.5cm x 46cm (14in x 18in) cushion pads.

The hedgehog cushion

From the yellow fabric cut a rectangle 32cm x 84cm (12½in x 33in). Mark the centre lines in both directions.

From the mauve fabric cut out the hedgehog's body and from the pink check fabric cut out the bristles.

Using a pencil, lightly mark the eye on his face.

Lay the yellow fabric with the short sides to your left and right and apply the pieces so that the animal is in the centre of the right hand half.

Sew the pieces to the ground fabric using pink thread.

From a scrap of white fabric mark the total area of the eye. Cut around, leaving a margin of 1.3cm (½in). On a piece of pink check fabric, mark the area of the eye pupil and cut around, leaving a small margin.

Place the white fabric in position and sew in place by hand, using small buttonhole stitches. Trim off the excess fabric. Sew the pupil in the same way.

Finish the cushion as for the elephant using the 30.5cm x 40.5cm (12in x 16in) cushion pad.

The camels cushion

From the red and white striped fabric, cut two rectangles 31.7cm x 77.5cm (12½in x 30½in).

From the remaining yellow fabric cut out the camels as for the elephant.

Lay out one of the red and white striped pieces and place the camels so that there is an equal margin all around the edge. Iron in the same way as before.

Sew the pieces to the ground fabric using red thread.

Lightly mark the features of the faces with pencil and then embroider them in stem stitch using two strands of the red thread. Use a large chain stitch for the eye of the baby camel.

Finish the cushion by placing the two pieces of striped fabric together with right sides facing. Sew around on three sides taking 1.3cm (½in) turnings. Turn through to right side and insert the remaining 30.5cm x 76.2cm (12in x 30in) cushion pad. Turn under the raw edges of the opening and slip-stitch.

Right *Use the outlines of the animals as a guide for transferring the shapes on to adhesive transfer paper. You may wish to make other animal shapes, if so, cut the motifs from books or magazines, and trace their outlines on graph paper.*

Novelty candy cushions

Make yourself some delicious candy cushions. Patterns for two sorts of chocolate and a bonbon are given here, but you can easily adapt them.

Cushion pads. In the instructions for the chocolate cushions the filling is placed directly inside the satin cover, which means it is not removable. If you prefer you can make a separate cushion pad to go inside the satin cover, making the pieces of the pad cover 1.3cm (½in) larger all around than the outer cover.

To make the rose petal chocolate cushion

You will need:

1.4m (1½yd) of 91.4cm (36in) wide brown satin for the 'chocolate'.

46cm (½yd) of 91.4cm (36in) wide pink satin for the rose petals.

1kg–1.35kg (2lb–3lb) kapok or use a synthetic filling for stuffing cushion.

46cm (½yd) of 61cm (24in) 55grm (2oz) synthetic wadding (batting) for rose petals.

Strong fabric adhesive.

Matching thread.

2.5m (2½yd) of 122cm (48in) wide lining

fabric (optional).
Make paper patterns for the cushions and the rose petals by enlarging figs. 1–4. Allow 1.3cm (½in) for seams.
Cut out four cushion top pieces and one cushion base piece in brown satin on the straight grain.
Cut out two of each petal section in pink satin, and one of each in 55gm (2oz) wadding (batting).

Place two cushion top pieces with right sides facing and stitch together on one side only from A–B. Join the other two pieces in the same way. Snip 'V'-shaped notches at 2.5cm (1in) intervals along the curved edges, almost to the stitching.

Place these two pieces together and stitch along the remaining two side seams. Press seams open.

With right sides together pin the base piece into place, matching the corners of the base to the seams of the top. Stitch the base to the top leaving one side open to turn through. (Leave two sides open if you have made a cushion pad.)

Trim corners and turn cushion to right side.

Insert filling until the cushion is firm (or insert the pad). Then slip stitch the opening.

Place the satin pieces for the larger petal section with right sides together on top of the wadding (batting) section. Tack (baste) and stitch through all thicknesses, all around the edge. Trim the wadding (batting) away close to the stitching and trim the seam allowance on the satin to 6mm (¼in).

Make clips into the edge, at the angles, almost to the stitching.

In the upper thickness of satin only, cut slits as shown (fig. 5). Turn the petals right side out.

Work lines of top stitching to make four petals (fig. 6).

Make up the smaller petal section in the same way and add three more lines of top stitching on each petal (fig. 7).

Glue the two petal sections together at the centre with the slit side of the smaller

1. *Cushion top piece – cut 4*
2. *Cushion base piece – cut 1*
3. *Lower petal section.* **4.** *Upper petal section. Cut two of each in satin and one of each in interfacing.*

Below *Close-up of the petals showing the stitching details.*

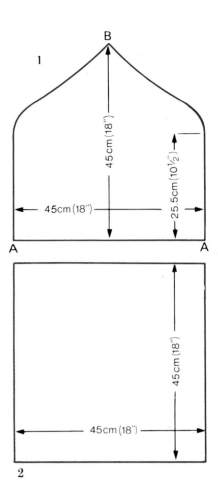

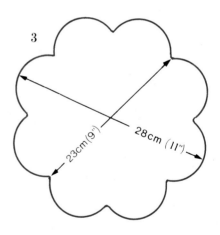

5 Above *Detail showing slits cut in the upper thickness.*

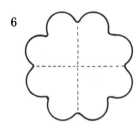

6 Above *Lines of topstitching to make four petals.*

7 Above *Further lines of topstitching are shown on the smaller petals.*

section to the unslit side of the larger one, making sure that the slits are completely covered. Stitch the two sections together at the centre.

Glue the larger petal section to the centre of the top of the cushion, covering the slits. Turn back the petals and stitch to the cushion at several points close to the glued centre.

To make the almond chocolate cushion

You will need:

91.4cm (1yd) of 91.4cm (36in) wide brown satin for the 'chocolate'.

34cm (⅜yd) of 91.4cm (36in) wide cream satin for the 'almond'.

About 1kg (2lb) kapok or a synthetic filling for cushion and almond.

Strong fabric adhesive (optional).

Matching thread.

91.4cm (1yd) of 91.4cm (36in) wide lining fabric (optional).

Make paper patterns for the cushion and

almond by enlarging figs. 8–11. Seam allowances of 1.3cm (½in) included on pattern.

Cut out two cushion side sections and two top/bottom cushion sections in brown satin.

Cut one of each almond section in cream satin.

With right sides together join the side strips at one end.

Work a line of stitches on stitch line on long edges and make notches 2.5cm (1in) apart almost to the stitching along both edges of side piece. This will help ease the fabric around curves when the side is joined to the top and bottom section.

With right sides together, and matching point C to the seam in the side section, tack (baste) and stitch the top/bottom section to the side section and join the other side seam, so that it matches point D, as for a round cushion with a welt. Attach the other top/bottom section in the same way but leave 25cm (10in), (45.7cm (18in) if a cushion pad is used) opening to turn through. Make 'V' notches at 2.5cm (1in) intervals all around the edge of the top and bottom sections.

Turn the cushion to the right side.

Insert the filling until the cushion is firm and slip stitch the opening.

Stitch ten 3mm (⅛in) pin tucks across the right side of the top almond section at

Above *Aerial view of almond chocolate, showing the lines of pin tucks.*

8. *Cushion side section – cut 2*
9. *Cushion top/bottom section – cut 2*
10. *Bottom of almond – cut 1*
11. *Top of almond – cut 1*

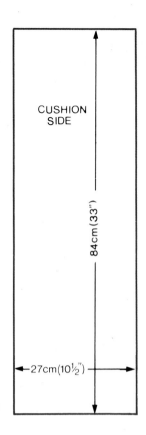

8 CUSHION SIDE
84cm (33")
27cm (10½")

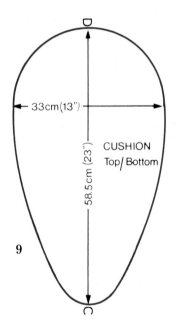

9 CUSHION Top/Bottom
33cm (13")
58.5cm (23")

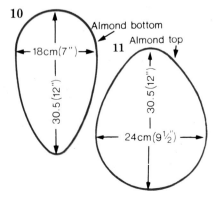

10 18cm (7")
30.5 (12")
Almond bottom
Almond top
11 30.5 (12")
24cm (9½")

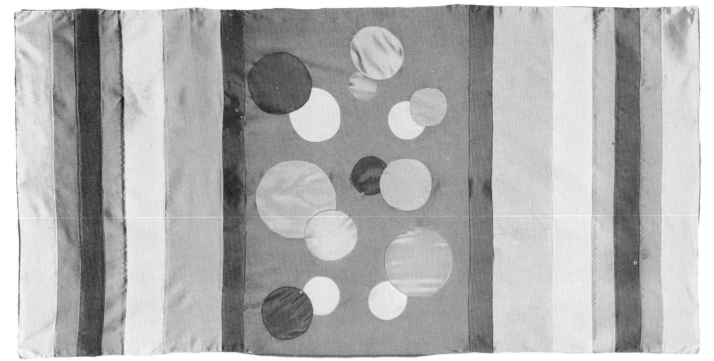

equal intervals, making the first and last tucks 3.2cm (1¼in) from the edge.

With right sides together stitch the top and bottom almond sections together, all round the edge.

Cut slits in the bottom section only as for the rose petals, trim turnings to 6mm (¼in) and turn the almond through to the right side. Stuff firmly with wadding (batting) and attach to the top of the cushion in the same way as the rose petals.

To make 'bonbon' cushion

This is made from a bolster with an outer cover made in one flat piece which is then wrapped around the bolster and tied with ribbon.

You will need:

For the bolster: 1.6m (1¾yd) cotton fabric.

1–1.5kg (2–2½lb) kapok or a synthetic filling, or a foam bolster pad 76cm (30in) long with a 23cm (9in) diameter.

For the cover: 91.4cm (1yd) of 91.4cm (36in) wide orange satin.

1.8m (2yd) of 91.4cm (36in) wide green satin.

45cm (½yd) of 91.4cm (36in) wide pink satin.

69cm (¾yd) of 91.4cm (36in) wide blue satin.

69cm (¾yd) of 91.4cm (36in) wide blue satin.

69cm (¾yd) of 91.4cm (36in) wide yellow satin.

1m (1¼yd) iron-on interfacing.

2 x 91.4cm (1yd) lengths of 1.3cm (½in) blue satin ribbon.

Matching thread.

Above *Bright satin stripes and circles compose the flat piece.*

Make up a bolster 76cm (30in) long and with a diameter of 23cm (9in).

Cut out strips of orange satin, from selvedge to selvedge of the fabric as follows: 2 x 8cm (3in) wide, pink; 2 x 18cm (7in) wide, blue; 4 x 13cm (5in) wide, yellow; 4 x 9cm (3½in) wide, green; and 2 x 62cm (24½in) wide, green (to line the striped ends).

Make circular paper patterns in a range of diameters between 18cm (3in) and 20cm (8in). Cut out in satin so that you have 4 blue, 4 yellow, 3 green and 3 pink circles.

Position the circles, right side up, on the wide orange strip as shown in the photograph. Tack (baste) into place and stitch in place with a fairly small zig zag stitch.

Note: The circles can be attached with a straight stitch but it will be necessary to turn under a very small hem all around before stitching.

Taking 1.3cm (½in) turnings join the narrow strips on either side of the broad orange one in the order shown in the photograph.

Trim turnings to 6mm (¼in) and press on the darker colour in each case.

Cut two pieces of interfacing 56cm x 91.4cm (22in x 36in) and iron one piece on to each end on the wrong side of the stripes, matching one long edge of the interfacing to the raw edge of the satin (the interfacing will reach only as far as the seam between the blue and pink stripes).

Make one raw edge neat on each 62cm x 91.4cm (24½ x 36in) green satin strip.

With right sides together place one green strip to one striped end, matching raw edges and selvedges. Tack (baste) and stitch around the three outer edges leaving the neat edge of green lining free. Trim corners and turn right side out. Work a line of straight stitching through all thicknesses along the seam between the blue and pink stripes to secure the fourth edge of the facing. Work the other end in the same way.

Press 1.3cm (½in) selvedge to the wrong side on the central unfaced section of the cover. Turn in about 6mm (¼in) and slip stitch down to make a neat finish.

Wrap the cover around the bolster and tie the ends with ribbon.

Above *You can really eat these chocolates, but our cushions look good enough to eat.*

59

Silk patchwork cushions

These beautiful silk cushions are an exquisite example of how patchwork can be worked to look both subtle and delicate. They are made up of traditional hexagonal shapes and the colours have been arranged to form a pattern of subtle pastel shades. Alternatively, brightly coloured patches can be arranged at random for a more modern look.

You will need:
Cushion pads.
Large bag of silk fabric scraps in different plain colours.
Silk fabric in harmonizing colour to cover the cushion.
Pre-shrunk piping cord.
Stiff card.
Paper.

It is important to select the colours for each cushion carefully. Use either three different colours in equal proportions, or four different colours, making one predominant, to tone with the colour scheme of the room.

For a really elegant effect, select the silk fabric in shades that are close to each other in tone.

If using slubbed or grained silk, work the patches so that they lie with the grain running in opposite ways to reflect the light in different directions.

To make the patches
The fabric shapes are cut out using a template, and then backed with paper to keep them firm while they are being stitched.

Templates can be purchased, but they can also be made quite satisfactorily from stiff cardboard. To make patches the same size as those illustrated, trace off the hexagonal shape given here and cut it out from cardboard.

Make two templates, one exactly to the size given and the other 6mm ($\frac{1}{4}$in) larger all around. The smaller is for cutting the paper shapes, the larger for cutting the fabric pieces, with a seam allowance all around. The backing used for the patches should be of fairly stiff paper, to keep them firm while working. Magazine covers or old greeting cards are suitable for this.

To prepare the patches
Cut out paper and fabric shapes.
There are approximately 8–10 hexagons along each edge of the patchwork square, but this can be varied according to the size of the cushion.
It is advisable to work out both the size and the colour arrangement beforehand on a sheet of graph paper. In this way it is possible to work out exactly how many shapes of each colour are required, remembering that the template shape given here is the exact size of the finished patch. Pin a paper shape to the wrong side of a fabric patch, placing the paper so that the turnings are exactly equal on all sides. Fold the turnings over the paper, pulling the fabric to the patch. Do not tie a knot in the thread, but simply tack (baste) the paper in place and remove the pins (fig. 1). Prepare the required number of patches in the same way.

Joining the patches
Patches can be joined by straight machine stitching (fig. 2a) or by hand. To join patches by hand, place two backed patches together, right sides facing, with edges carefully matched. Stitch along one edge, using a fine needle and matching thread (fig. 2b). Never pull an edge to fit if it does not match up, but unpick the patch and begin again. When all the patches are stitched together, press the work lightly on the wrong side. Snip the tacking (basting) threads, pull them out, then remove the paper backing.

To make up
Make a piped cushion cover from plain silk fabric in one of the colours used to make the patchwork. Cover the cushion, and either stitch together the final seam or insert a zipper.
Lay the finished patchwork on one side of the cushion and stitch neatly in place.

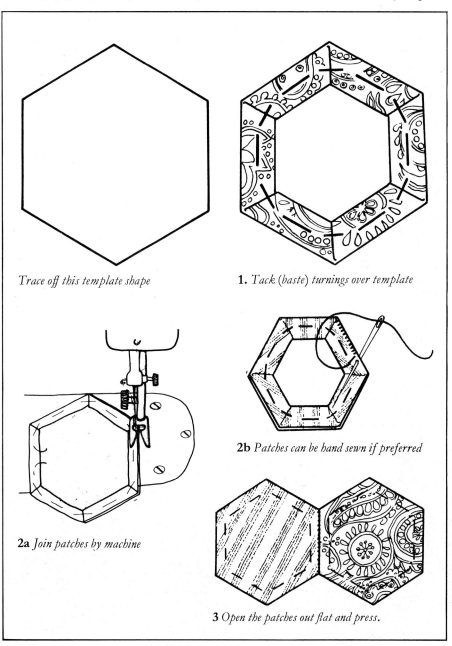

Trace off this template shape

1. *Tack (baste) turnings over template*

2a *Join patches by machine*

2b *Patches can be hand sewn if preferred*

3 *Open the patches out flat and press.*

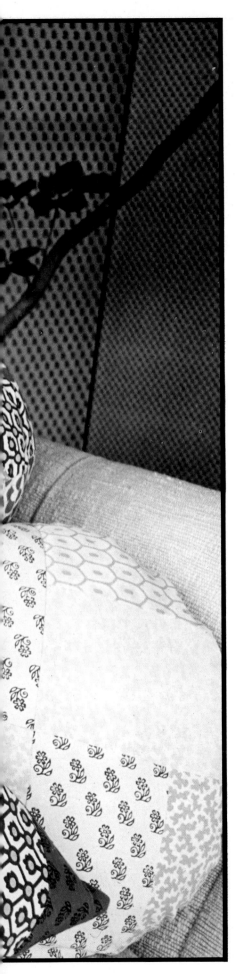

Cushions from scraps

Use the prettiest left over pieces in your sewing box to make these simple cushions.

Simple patchwork

Patchwork is the old craft of using up scraps of fabric by joining them in an attractive way. These cushions are made in the simplest and quickest form of patchwork where the fabric is cut into squares or oblongs, because these can be machine stitched together unlike more complicated shapes which have to be hand sewn.

The fabric

It is normally best not to mix old and new fabrics in a piece of work because they will wear unevenly. For the same reason it is advisable not to mix fabrics of different fibres, nylon and cotton for example, or of different weights, such as denim and lawn.

The design

The squares can all be cut to the same size and joined in strips, or you can combine squares and oblongs in different sizes. If you choose the former method,

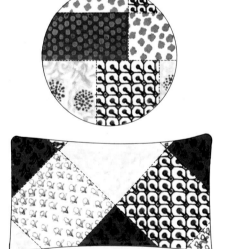

Left *You can make attractive cushions like these with spare fabric scraps.*

the sewing must be accurate so that all the joins meet. With the latter method, you should plan your design carefully on paper first as this will simplify cutting the patches. To plan your design, use graph paper marked with 2.54cm (1in) squares, and draw on the shape of the overall finished item reducing it proportionally if necessary.

For square patches, between 5cm–15.3cm (2in–6in) are the most practical size. For oblong patches, it is normally most effective if you make the short sides between 5cm–10.1cm (2in–4in) and the longer sides between 10.1cm–15.3cm (4in–6in).

Making the patches

Cut or tear the patches along the grain of the fabric, allowing 6mm ($\frac{1}{4}$in) all around for turnings. If you are making all oblong patches they can be joined in a brick pattern, so that the vertical seams on each alternative row come to the centre of the patches in the row on each side. For this, you will also have to cut half-width patches to fill in the spaces at each end of alternate rows.

Joining the patches

Where possible, join the patches into strips for the horizontal rows first, then join the strips together for the vertical rows.

If you are experienced with a machine, there is no need to tack (baste) the patches together first if you put the pins at right-angles to the edge so that the machine foot can ride over them. Where it is essential to have accurate joins, pin these first and then put in the intermediate pins. Press the turnings open after completing each strip.

Finishing off

For cushion covers the patchwork need not be finished off in any special way because the turnings of the seams will be hidden inside.

Estimating cushions
Plain cushion cover

For a good fit, cover should be slightly smaller all around than cushion pad. For a 45.7cm (18in) square cushion with piped edges you would need 107.9cm (1$\frac{1}{8}$yds) of 91.4cm (36in) fabric or 57.1cm ($\frac{5}{8}$yd) of 121.9cm (48in) fabric. The cutting diagrams include fabric for bias, strips for piping and 1.3cm ($\frac{1}{2}$in) seams, so allow correspondingly less for an unpiped cover. Measure perimeter of cushion to find amount of piping cord (pre-shrunk).

Useful accessories

Useful accessories

The success of any job depends upon choice of tools. Having the right tools makes your work easier, quicker and more enjoyable.

You will need

A sewing machine There are three main types: straight stitch, swing needle (zig-zag), and swing needle automatic.

Straight stitch. This type will sew only in a straight line. It is the least expensive and is perfectly adequate for basic sewing. It is also possible to buy attachments, such as a piping foot for stitching close to a zipper.

Swing needle. As well as straight stitching this machine does zig-zag stitching which is useful for finishing seams and hems, for making buttonholes for stitching stretch fabrics, and for sewing on buttons. It is also possible to do simple embroidery stitches. Swing needle machines are in the medium price bracket.

Swing needle automatic. This machine does embroidery as well as the stitches which the other two types offer. But this type of machine is the most expensive and rather a luxury unless you intend to do a good deal of decorative stitching and embroidery.

Note Make sure that the machine you buy has a clear instruction book. It is also important, particularly with a more complex machine, to have it explained by an expert and if possible to take a few short lessons in its use. In order to get the best possible results, it is essential to get to know your machine really well.

Machine needles Use size 70–80 (11–12) for medium fabrics, size 80–90 (12–14) for heavy cottons and blended cloth, and size 100–110 (16–18) for heavy coatings and plastic. Continental sizes are given first here followed by British sizes in brackets.

Ballpoint machine needles should be used for jersey fabrics to prevent cutting the thread and runs in the fabric.

Sewing needles Use size 8 or 9 for most fabrics, size 6 or 7 for fabrics such as heavy linen and for stitching on buttons, and size 10 for fine work.

Pins Use steel dressmaking pins, at least 2.54cm (1in) long. Nickel-plated pins sometimes bend during use and could damage fine cloth. Glasshead pins are very sharp but have limited use as the heads easily break.

Tape measure Buy one with centimetre and inch markings. The fibre glass type is the best as it will not stretch. One with a metal strip attached at one end is useful, especially when taking up hems.

Thread For man-made fibres use a synthetic thread. Linens and cottons require either mercerized cotton or silk, 50.

For woollen fabrics use either a silk or synthetic thread as the cloth has a certain amount of elasticity and the thread should have the same quality.

With all types of thread the higher the number given on the label, the finer the thread.

Scissors Small shears, 17.8cm – 20.3cm (7–8in) long are best for cutting out most fabrics as they are heavier than scissors and glide through the cloth more easily. Larger shears are advisable when making up heavy fabrics. The handles should comfortably fit the hand (left-handed shears are available).

Small scissors are useful for clipping seams and threads.

Stitch picker This is better than scissors for cutting machine-made buttonholes, and for removing buttons and snap fasteners, as well as being useful for un-picking. Various types are available at most haberdashers.

Iron It is necessary to have a good medium-weight iron with thermostatic controls. If you use a steam iron you must use distilled water.

Ironing board An essential item for pressing seams flat. It should stand firmly and have a smooth-fitting cover. A sleeve board is useful.

Pressing cloth A piece of finely woven cotton or lawn, 61cm (2ft) square, is essential for steam pressing. Your cloth should not have holes, frayed edges or prominent grains, as these can leave an impression on the fabric being pressed. Nor should the cloth contain any dressing as this will stick to the iron and mark the fabric.

Tailor's chalk Have two pieces for marking your fabric, white for dark fabrics and dark for light fabrics.

Tracing Wheel Use this for marking pattern outlines onto fabric. One made from steel with sharp points is best.

Thimble This should fit the middle finger of your sewing hand. Choose a metal one as the needle can penetrate through a plastic one while sewing.

Pinking shears Not essential but useful to give a neater finish to seams, particularly when working with knitted and non-fraying fabrics.

Choosing fabrics

Always check when purchasing whether a fabric can be hand-washed or must be dry cleaned. If in doubt, wash a small test piece before making up. This is especially necessary when making a garment in two different coloured fabrics or when using a loosely woven fabric.

To find out whether a fabric is colourfast wash a small square about 7.5cm (3in) square. Press while still damp onto some white fabric. The colour will run onto the white fabric if it is not colourfast.

To test for shrinkage measure a similar square of fabric, or draw around it, before washing and measure again when when dry and then compare the two.

INDEX